Classic Golf Tips

By TOMMY ARMOUR

Foreword by Tommy Armour III

CONTEMPORARY BOOKS

A TRIBUNE NEW MEDIA COMPANY

Library of Congress Cataloging-in-Publication Data

Armour, Tommy.
    Classic golf tips / by Tommy Armour.
        p.   cm.
    Originally published: Orlando : Tribune Pub.,
c1994.
    ISBN 0-8092-3342-8 (alk. paper)
    1. Golf.   I. Title.
GV965.A73   1995
796.352—dc20   95-23058
                                        CIP

Published by Contemporary Books, Inc.
Two Prudential Plaza, Chicago, Illinois 60601-6790
Manufactured in the United States of America
International Standard Book Number: 0-8092-3342-8
10   9   8   7   6   5   4   3   2   1

CONTENTS

FOREWORD

It is an honor and a privilege to write the foreword to a book of my grandfather's teachings. While fate did not allow me the chance to get to know him well (he died when I was just eight years old), I have always felt an incredibly strong bond to Tommy Armour. In addition to carrying his name, which will always hold a place of great distinction in the history of golf, I like to think I've been the beneficiary of some of his physical and mental gifts, as well as a competitive fire that is hard to describe. I only know that since I was a little boy I wanted to become a golf professional and to compete at the highest level, just as he did.

Some of the stories related here come from my father, Dr. Thomas Armour, a general surgeon in Las Vegas. My dad was at one time a good enough golfer to win three consecutive club championships at the Desert Inn, but he likes to joke that the golfing talent in our family skipped a generation. To those who inquire about his decision to pursue medicine rather than a golf career, he says, "I'm a scratch surgeon. And that's all I ever really wanted to be."

I've played a few years on the European Tour, in addition to my eight years on the PGA Tour, and everywhere I go I'm approached by people who saw my grandfather play, or took lessons from him, or in some cases even claim to have caddied for him in tournaments. When the caddie claim is made by a man in his 50s, I have to be suspicious, seeing that grandfather quit playing tournament golf in the 1930s. But I usually just smile and thank them for the memory.

I know they mean well. Whenever I'm convinced that the person is sincere, and did in fact know Tommy Armour, I feel a twinge of jealousy. I sure wish I could have gotten to know him better. He was an incredibly talented and eclectic man who had a hearty appetite for the finer things in life.

In addition to his golfing prowess and his reputation as the best golf instructor of his day, he was a bridge master, an outstanding billiards player, a boxing aficionado, a savvy bettor at the racetrack and, as Byron Nelson recently told me, "Armour was absolutely the most gifted storyteller I've ever known in golf. He could take the worst story you ever heard and make it great."

I hope I can do my grandfather justice by telling a few stories about him.

Tommy Armour was born in Edinburgh, Scotland, and was first taught to play by his oldest brother, Sandy, who was good enough to win the Scottish Amateur championship. Tommy caddied for Sandy in the final round, and on the last green he was so excited by the victory that he got rattled and stuck Sandy's putter in the hole and put the flagstick in the golf bag. That actually happened, because grandfather confessed the *faux pas* to an American writer years later.

Once he started to win tournaments in Scotland and England, Tommy was taken under the wing of Harry Vardon, who at that time was the most venerated player/instructor in the world.

One of my grandfather's boyhood companions was Bobby Cruickshank, who years later was good enough to win several tournaments on the American tour and was twice runner-up in the U.S. Open. Cruickshank and Sandy Armour were taken prisoner by the Germans in the First World War, and Bobby nearly died of dysentery. He required extra portions of food, which Sandy was able to get from the German officers by entertaining them with his violin. Cruickshank and my grandfather were great friends throughout their lives, and they became legendary in the 1920s and '30s for exploits both on and off the course.

They once missed catching a train because they were "detained" in the 19th hole after a tournament, so their wives left without them. An hour after departure the train was halted by a car stalled on the tracks, and Armour and Cruickshank jovially boarded as if nothing were out of the ordinary.

Like all great players, Tommy Armour combined his physical gifts – strong, quick hands and an uncanny sense of rhythm and timing – with a mental toughness and ability to focus under pressure to become one of the best players of his time. During a five-year stretch, from 1927 to 1931, he won 16 tournaments, including the U.S. Open, the PGA, the British Open, the Western Open and two Canadian Opens. He won more than 40 tournaments in all. His strength was driving the ball long and straight, and he was a superb iron player. He was not a great putter, perhaps because of his problems with depth perception, the result of losing an eye in battle in World War I. But he was a great clutch putter. His three major championships were won either by one stroke or in a playoff, and in each case he made tough pressure putts on the final holes.

Because of his vision problem, Armour was one of the first players to chart yardages on the course. He even went to the extent of memorizing hole layouts and terrain changes. He was extremely deliberate around the greens, often sighting the line of a putt four or five times before stroking it. He once missed an important putt on the final hole of a tournament by aiming his putt at a distant ship. The problem was that between the time he originally lined up the putt and when he hit it, the ship had pulled out of the harbor.

Later in life, Armour enjoyed playing team matches for a few dollars. He and Bobby Jones were nearly unbeaten as partners, and down in Boca Raton, Florida, he often teamed with the great amateur Frank Stranahan and with Julius Boros, who was one of his prize pupils. One of the first times Armour played with Boros was in a casual nine-hole round, in which Armour was asked to evaluate Boros' game. When they were finished, Julius looked at him with disappointment and said, "You didn't give me any pointers."

Armour just shrugged and said, "If I had a short game like yours, I wouldn't give a damn where I hit it."

Tommy was never one to mince words. Once when he was

giving my father a lesson, Dad asked him why he was having so much trouble getting a feel for the proper golf swing. Grandfather told him, "You have dumb muscles."

Shortly after my mother and father married, she played a round of golf with her new father-in-law at Winged Foot Golf Club. On one hole her ball landed in a deep bunker, and she took three flails at the ball without getting over the lip. Armour sauntered over to her and, with his customary directness, said, "Little lady, why don't you just turn around and chip it out backwards. You'll finish the hole a lot quicker."

While she found him to be intimidating, mother says he was a great teacher and the most dynamic person she'd ever been around. He gave her a short-game pointer later on – to try to master chipping with a 7-iron, and to use it whenever possible from off the green – and his advice helped her lower her handicap to three.

Another time, he was asked to give a lesson to a wealthy golfer who had taken up the game primarily for the social benefits. He watched the man hit a dozen or so shots. The duffer was slapping away at it, feeling pretty good about his progress, when he finally turned to Armour for an evaluation. "Well, what d'ya think?" he said.

"I think you should give it up," Armour said, and walked away.

From all accounts, Tommy Armour had no patience with people who played golf just to be in vogue. He wanted to help only those who had a desire to improve and were willing to practice what he taught them.

Armour also was intolerant of people who put others down. My father recalls vividly how he was put in his place one day. I'll let Dad tell the story first-hand:

"I was about 11 years old and my father took me to a Yankees game. It was a memorable day for several reasons. We sat in a box seat near home plate and I was introduced to Babe Ruth, who was a friend of Dad's and one of his golf pupils. On the way to the park, I asked Dad who the Yankees were playing, and he told me the Cleveland Indians. Now back then, the Indians were near the bottom of the league, and I said, 'Ah, they're a bunch of bums.'

"Dad spun on me and said, 'Son, don't ever call a professional athlete who has reached the majors a bum. Every one of those guys is an outstanding player just to be in the big leagues. Never use that term.'

"Well, I shrank into my seat, and sure enough the Indians hammered the Yankees, 14-3. From that time on, I've always rooted for the Cleveland Indians."

Here's another recollection from my father:

"Whenever Dad sat around in the clubhouse at Boca Raton, it was as though he were holding court. A crowd would gather just to listen to his stories. The waitress always knew to bring over a large tray with several cocktails, usually gin and ginger ale with a bourbon chaser, which he would follow with a Bromo Seltzer. People would look at that tray and their eyes would grow wider. Once Errol Flynn and Bruce Cabot, two of the more notorious ladies' men of their time, dropped by to visit Dad when I was there, and every head turned. Those guys had the look of the eagle when they scanned the room. You got the feeling they were undressing every woman in the place.

"One time Babe Didrikson was at Dad's table. She was a student of his, and he had the utmost respect for her. Dad thought Babe was the greatest athlete – male or female – of her time. There was also a member of the club at the table, a particularly wealthy man, who noticeably snubbed Babe when he was introduced to her. When she left, my father said to him, 'Ya know, you were rather rude to Mildred. Do you have something against her?'

"And the man replied, 'No, I just find her rather crude.'

"Dad glared at him and said, 'How can any Irishman look at that wonderful woman and say she's crude? I just can't believe it.'

"The table went totally silent, and the man stood up and left. It seemed like an hour before somebody finally cleared their throat and the conversation resumed. It was the only time I'd ever heard Dad say something about another man's heritage, but it was only to retaliate for the man's rudeness. He was the most unprejudiced person I've ever known."

My father also has opinions about the legacy his father has passed on to me:

"My son has the same big, strong hands as his grandfather. And Tommy has Dad's ability to bite his lower lip and keep plugging when things are tough. Tommy also is polite and sympathetic toward fans seeking autographs and conversation, which was a characteristic of his grandfather.

"If Dad were here today to watch Tommy play, I think he'd work with him on making more of a pause at the top of his backswing. He'd spend a lot of time talking to him about rhythm and timing, but I also think he'd be pleased with Tommy's success as a professional golfer, just as he was proud of my career in medicine."

Perhaps one other thing passed down from my grandfather is a flair for nice clothing. Byron Nelson told me, "Your grandfather was always meticulously dressed. I never remember seeing him look anything but dapper, and he never had a hair out of place."

My philosophy has always been this: Look good; feel good; play good. *Sports Illustrated* had some fun with my preoccupation with fashion in 1990, when they did a three-part feature on the golf boom in America. They cited the "Fifty Nifty Reasons to Feel Good About Golf." Reason number 4 was: "Tommy Armour III, grandson of the Silver Scot himself. Armour wears long-sleeved cotton shirts with the top button fastened. He wears Giorgio Armani slacks, baggy and pleated. He has longish hair and likes rock music, and yet, to golf's surprise, is not a member of the Communist Party. He can also flat-out play. He has already won at Phoenix this year. Armour is to cool golf what Gerald Ford was to dork golf."

I'd like to think that my grandfather would approve.

There are several reasons why Tommy Armour was a great golf

instructor, most of which you'll find reflected in this book. My dad says it was because he was such an analytical thinker. He could truly understand the combination of physics and athleticism that good golfing requires.

Byron Nelson says that in addition to his great understanding of the swing, my grandfather was a master of psychology when he was teaching. "He could talk people into believing they could play better," Byron told me. "He would give his students a lot of encouragement and positive thoughts, and he would build their confidence."

When you consider the number of outstanding players he taught, players such as Babe Didrikson Zaharias, Julius Boros, Ralph Guldah, Lawson Little, Betty Jameson and Peggy Kirk Bell, and the thousands of casual golfers he helped improve, it's obvious that his gifts as a teacher equaled his talents as a player.

Tommy Armour will always be remembered as a professional golfer who could do it all, both on and off the course. I hope you enjoy his insights in the following pages, and I hope some of his wisdom rubs off on me as I try to emulate his wonderful qualities as a golfer and as a person.

Good luck and good golfing.

Tommy Armour III
August 1993

THE
GRIP

POSITIVE THINKING

When I got a bad shot while I was playing championship golf I corrected my error by positive thinking. I didn't wonder what I was doing wrong but concentrated on what I knew I must do right. I stress the same policy in my teaching. I get my pupils, including you, doing what they should do instead of wasting their mental energy on futile post-mortems.

Feel

Hold

A very important thing to do right is to have the right-hand grip of the club light and principally with the middle two fingers. The tips of those fingers are the gripping points, without stiffening the right arm. The right forefinger hooked in a trigger-finger position, with the club against the fattest third of the finger – keeping the thumb tip at about a 1 o'clock position on the shaft – is the correct position for feeling the club.

KEEP THINKING

Practice is a fascinating part of golf for the golfer who uses his brain. But you've got to keep thinking! It takes a lot of thinking and feeling to develop the habit of holding the club a little firmer with the last three fingers of the left hand, rather than responding to an instinctive urge to hold with a stronger right-hand grip (if you're right-handed). Accenting the right hand of the coupling at address will have you lifting the club away from the ball instead of swinging

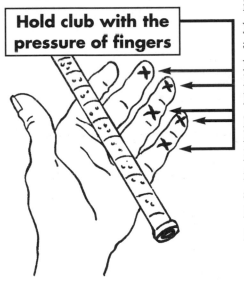

Hold club with the pressure of fingers

it away with your left arm and hand as you should. Every time you hit a shot in practice, study how your hands and fingers are arranged and how the finger pressures feel.

WATCH THAT GRIP

When you hear a feeble thud instead of a smart crack as you strike the ball, the weakness is in your grip. Probably your hands are not working closely together to hold the club firmly but flexibly so

Hands close together

it can be whipped into the shot. Make sure that the butt of your right thumb fits snugly over your left thumb. With the tips of the last three fingers of your left hand and the middle two fingers of your right hand, press the club against the roots of your fingers. With this finger grip your wrists can hinge correctly and easily.

PLANNED PROCEDURE

A ny time, any place, is good for starting the habit of making your golf shots by planned procedure. The ordinary golfer repeats his good methods by accident rather than by design. You can start right now to put your golf into good order. The place to start is with the connection between yourself and your club. The ordinary player's grip usually is too stiff because it is too much in the palms of his hands and too tight. Feel that your club is held mainly by gentle but firm pressure from the tips of the last three fingers of your left hand and the middle two of your right hand.

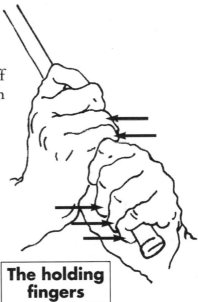

The holding fingers

Sensitive Feel

Always be careful about your grip. Notice how the experts keep moving their fingers on the club as they address the ball. That is so they get the correct position and a sensitive feel. When your grip is as it should be – mainly with the fingers – you almost can *think with your fingers.* You can subconsciously manipulate the club as your sense of touch and your muscular sense signal that the clubface position must be adjusted. Be certain that the Vs between your thumbs and forefingers are snug and firm so the club can't possibly slide down too much into the palms of your hands.

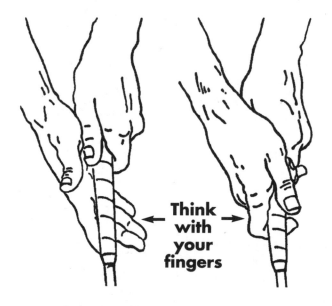

Think
your
fingers

FINGER CONNECTION

Hold the club gently with the fingers of your right hand. Get the sensation of feeling the weight and face position of the clubhead with the tips of your fingers. The strong part of your connection with the club is with the last three fingers of the left hand firmly hooking the grip against the heel of the hand. If the right-hand fingers are placed correctly you are sure to strengthen the grip instinctively when you get to the point where you begin whipping the right hand into the shot. The left hand works to guide the club reliably; the right hand provides the power.

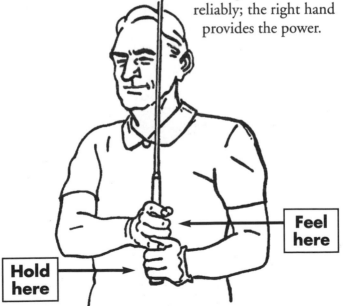

Feel here

Hold here

GRIP CONTROL

When you get into your head the big idea that you should whip the club into the shot and not pound or scoop the ball, you're beginning to get the picture of the type of connection the grip should be. Then you can understand why the grip must hold the club under secure but flexible control, primarily with the fingers and in such a way that the wrists always can work freely. The last three fingers of the left hand latch the club against the heel of the hand all through the swing. Pressure from those fingers is firm but not stiff. There is a lighter hold with the middle two fingers of the right hand.

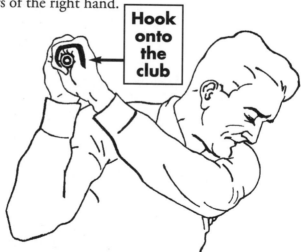

Hook onto the club

CHECK YOUR GRIP

Concentrate on your hands the next time you practice. First, check every detail of your grip. Is the club being held mainly by your fingers so the connection between you and the club is strong and flexible and your wrists can work freely? Remember: You whip the golf club into the shot, you don't pound with it. Are the Vs of your thumbs and forefingers snug so the club won't slide down into the palm of your hand? Are those Vs pointing to your right ear – normally the best position for the average golfer? Are your hands close together with the heel of the right thumb snugly over the left thumb?

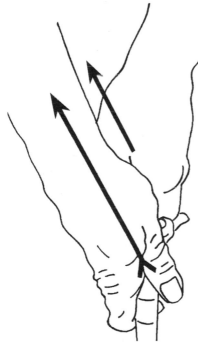

Hold the club like a whip

EXPERIMENT WITH GRIP

Intelligent experimenting instead of merely hitting shots gives you dividends from your practice time. Some very simple experiments work wonders, especially with your grip. Try slight changes in the angle of the grip from your hooked left forefinger across your other fingers. You've got a lot of leeway as long as you don't allow the shaft to fall into the palm of your hand. Discover just what position enables you to hold the club firmly with the last three fingers of your left hand without freezing your forearm muscles. You may discover, too, that even for the long shots gripping the club down a little from the cap of the shaft gives you a better feeling of control.

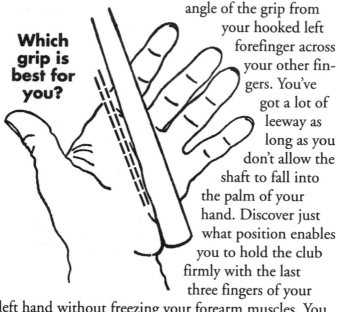

Which grip is best for you?

THE GRIP

Possibly the most valuable help I've given many golfers is teaching them how to practice. When I can get them *practicing and experimenting intelligently* they can then teach themselves a great deal of what they need to know individually. Most golfers are wasting time at what they think is practice. They fail to concentrate on one feature; for instance, the grip. The majority of average golfers hold the club so far down in the palm of the left hand that their wrist action is cramped. Thus, they cannot cock the club almost automatically at the top of the backswing or keep the left hand in control all through the swing.

Finger hold keeps wrists flexible

FINGER GRIP

There are two reasons for holding the golf club by your fingers rather than in the palms of your hands. One is that you need speed, *not brute force,* to manipulate the club. The strength you need is for controlling the clubface position. It is provided by the last three fingers of the left hand snugly securing the club against the heel of that hand. The other reason for gripping mainly with your fingers is that your wrists have to cock at the top of the backswing and uncock as you begin your hitting action. If your club is gripped in the palms of your hands, your wrist movement will be cramped and you can't get whip into the club.

Fingers hold the club

A GOOD GRIP

A good grip offsets many faults of the golfer. A great thing about the connection between player and club is that both hands work as though they are one. This unity can be assisted by having the left thumb on the shaft so it fits snugly in the hollow of the right thumb and palm. The butt of the right thumb should press firmly on the left thumb. The left thumb should be under the shaft and supporting it at the top of the backswing. The right forefinger should be hooked around the shaft in a sort of trigger-finger position and touching the thumb, but don't hold tight with these fingers.

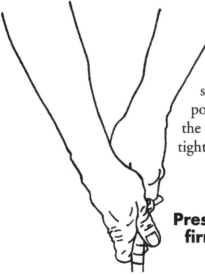

Press right thumb firmly onto left thumb

FINGER PRESSURE

Hold the club with firm (but not stiff) pressure from the tips of the last three fingers of your left hand. Angle the club from your crooked left forefinger to about the middle of the hand, so when you close your fingers around the club you've got it snugly against the heel of your hand. This grip gives you the flexibility you need for cocking your wrists. If you ever allow the club to slide down into the palm of your hand you will cramp the wrist action. The right-hand hold on the club is mainly with the middle two fingers. The thumb and right forefinger should be in a trigger-finger position on the club so they can work correctly.

Hold firm

KEEP IT SIMPLE

Simple methods of playing golf are the best. A multitude of confusing and unnecessary details beat most men and women out of the good games they want to play and easily could play. A good grip is a simple thing. Let your arms hang naturally close to your legs. Without rolling the wrist, move your left arm around so the shaft of the club is lying from your hooked left forefinger to the hollow between your left little finger and the heel of your palm. Place your left thumb on the shaft so the club won't slip down between the thumb and forefinger. Then close your fingers around the grip with a little pressure of the last three fingers securing the club against the heel of the hand. Now you've got your left hand set to guide the club.

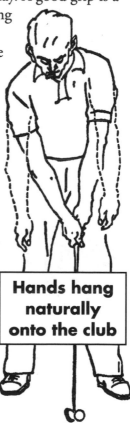

Hands hang naturally onto the club

HOLD CLUB CORRECTLY

The first thing to learn about playing good golf is a good grip. Many who call themselves golfers never have learned to hold a club correctly. They've got to get the habit of connecting themselves to the club mainly with finger pressure to be able to hit shots uniformly well. Pressure from the last three fingers of the left hand securing the club grip against the heel of the hand gives you a coupling that allows the hands to work properly and keeps the club under control without excessive tension. The left hand primarily is the part of the grip that guides the club. A lighter pressure from the middle two fingers of the right hand is the part of the coupling through which power is applied to whip the clubhead through the ball.

Here is control

WORK ON GRIP

Winter practice, by giving the average golfer the correct feel of the grip, the stance and the swing, is bound to improve a player's golf. Golfers seldom know the feel of a good shot. In the first place, they rarely feel that the club is being held with the tips of the last three fingers of the left hand and the middle two of the right hand, pressing snugly but not in a cramped way. Work on getting a grip that gives you the feeling the club can be whipped vigorously through the shot and will instinctively strengthen as the ball is hit.

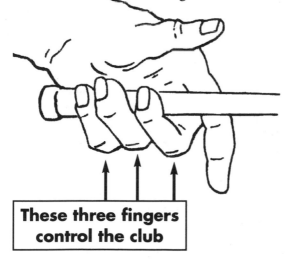

These three fingers control the club

COMPACT HANDS

For the essential feeling of "togetherness" of your hands in holding a golf club have your left thumb down the shaft in about a 1 o'clock position. Your right thumb has to be snugly over the left thumb. Both of your hands should feel that they form a compact coupling. The inner section of your right index finger is placed against the side of the shaft away from the target. That's a small but important detail of shot-making. It's that near section of the hooked right forefinger that has a great deal to do with speeding the clubhead so you get a fierce lash into it.

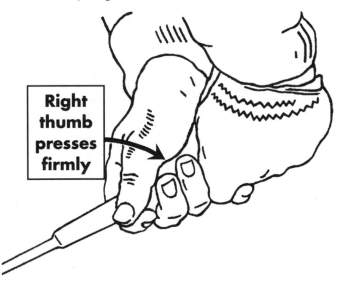

Right thumb presses firmly

EXAMINE GRIP

At the end of the golf year you ought to be subjecting yourself to an organized and thoughtful examination to determine whether you have good, sound golfing habits that will lead you to improvement or whether you're handicapped by faults in your grip, stance and swing. Your grip ought to be examined first. If you aren't scoring satisfactorily chances are 99 to 1 your grip is poor and the club comes loose in your hands. The cure is not to grab the club with a tight, tense grip but to make sure that it is held securely against the heel of your left hand by pressure from the fingertips of the last three fingers of that hand.

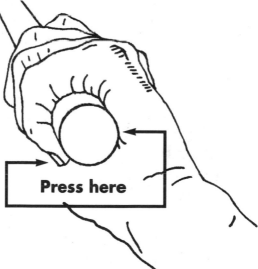

Press here

DON'T TURN WRIST

With the left hand holding the club so you can steer it correctly, simply move your right hand from where it is hanging naturally by your leg and fit it into the grip in a way that puts the left hand snugly against the right and the lifeline of the right hand against your left thumb. Don't turn your wrist. The V of your right thumb and forefinger points about to your right ear. The grip used by most golfers – experts and beginners – is the overlapping grip with the right little finger hooked over the left forefinger. That is the grip the great Harry Vardon popularized. It brings the hands together so they can work in close coordination. The right thumb and forefinger rest quite lightly on the shaft in a sort of trigger grip. The middle two fingers are the ones that make the main connection through which power is whipped into the shot by the right side.

Control

Power

LEFT HAND GUIDE

Keep your hands ahead of the clubhead as long as you can and you will hit quite satisfactory golf shots. This calls for leading the shot with a straight left arm, pulling the club down from the top of the backswing and refraining from unlocking your wrists until the last possible moment. It also means swinging the back of your left hand through the shot and well along the direction line until your body turns facing the hole and your right hand turns over the left in traveling toward a high follow-through. The left hand never should weaken as a guide even when the right is strongest in applying power.

Keep hands ahead

PRECISION AIM

Watch other golfers who don't score satisfactorily and see how many of their shots are incorrectly aimed. Learn from their carelessness in standing that you've got to have the bottom line of the clubface squarely across the line to the hole, then adjust your stance and posture so you can swing the club correctly toward the hole. That precision aim must be taken on every shot, from a short putt to your longest drive. Get the mental picture of the line from the target back to the face of your club. That way you can make more precise adjustments of stance, posture and grip than you can when you set yourself to the ball then try to shift around so you'll be accurately aimed.

Aim carefully

STANCE
&
SET UP

UNDERSTAND YOUR GOLF

In organizing your game so good golf becomes a habit instead of an accident you should understand the reason for the various types of stance. The open stance, with the left foot drawn back from the direction line and the body partially turned toward the hole, generally is used when you don't need much body action for the shot but will make it with your shoulders, arms and hands. The square stance, with feet equidistant from the direction line, is recommended for medium-distance shots when you need body turn as well as accuracy, and for short approaches of the putting stroke variety. The closed stance, with the right foot drawn back from the direction line, is usually used when a big body turn and a lot of distance are wanted.

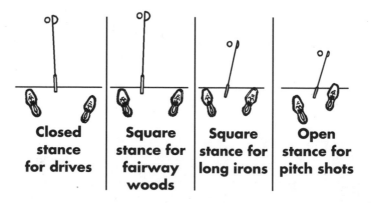

Closed stance for drives | **Square stance for fairway woods** | **Square stance for long irons** | **Open stance for pitch shots**

SIGHT THE SHOT

Carelessness in aiming a shot is the frequent and unpardonable sin of the average golfer who throws away a lot of strokes each round he plays. If he is ever going to improve, he has got to get himself into the good habit of tentatively placing the clubhead flat on the ground in back of the ball, then aiming the bottom leading edge of the club squarely across the direction line. Then he should adjust his feet, his posture and his grip so everything about him will be coordinated to whip the club into the shot with the face of the club striking the ball with at least a planned effort at precision.

CHECK STANCE

At least a hundred times a year I am sorely tempted to yell at a playing companion as he addresses the ball "Stop! Have you any idea where you're shooting?" If on certain holes you go out of bounds or into water or rough so much you think you are jinxed, why don't you try checking your stance now and then? Place your club at the tips of your toes and often you'll be amazed to learn that you actually are aiming at trouble. Aim carefully, then get and keep in your mind the idea that you are going to throw the clubhead along the direction line of your shot.

"Throw" club along direction line

Aim your feet

ADDRESSING THE BALL

Most golfers stand too far away from the ball as they address it. When you sole the club behind the ball and allow the angle and length of the club to determine your stance, you will find it much easier to swing back, then into and through the ball, without losing balance. Your hands should hang down comfortably close to your body. Your wrists at address should bend downward so there are no wrinkles showing. When you look down at your grip and see wrinkles in your wrists, chances are you are reaching for the ball and not using the club the way it was designed.

Angle and length of shaft show where to stand

Get Organized

You'll probably save time and strokes by waiting until you get yourself organized to make a good shot. Most ordinary golfers I see hurry so much they don't give themselves time to hold the club correctly, with the Vs of the thumbs and forefingers pointing about to the right ear. Then they rush instead of being careful about the relationship of their feet to the ball at address. They should address the ball no farther to the left than a line with the back of the left heel. Often they won't give the backswing enough time. They ought to swing back until the left shoulder touches the chin. So they hurry themselves into ruining easy shots.

Careful about the Vs

Ball always back of heel

TAKE AIM

"What went wrong with that shot, Tommy?" I'm asked by many of the average golfers with whom I play. They expect some highly technical answer and I disappoint them by telling them they simply didn't aim the shot with sense and care. A high percentage of shots are off line because the player didn't sole the club behind the ball and aim the club-face, his feet, body and hands precisely. For almost all average players, the Vs of the thumbs and forefingers should point at the right ear when the club is soled back of the ball. The left arm should be straight and the right elbow bent in fairly close to the ribs.

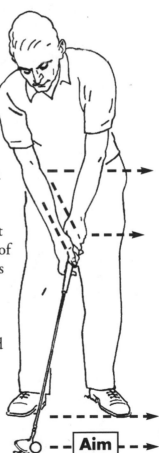

Aim

STAND KNOCK-KNEED

Turn your toes out a bit as you stand to the ball. That will help you turn your body more easily. Distribute your weight evenly between the balls of your feet and the heels and you won't be inclined to fall forward as you swing – a common error of the golfer who addresses the ball incorrectly. It's a good idea to stand a wee bit knock-kneed so your weight at address will be a trifle heavier on the inner edges of your shoes. Some very good golfers wiggle their toes as they address the ball. That reminds them to get a good stable foundation for the swing and to feel free for foot action.

Weight is even on toes and heels

FOOT PLACEMENT

A tendency of the average golfer is to place his feet too close together for the medium and long shots that require full and easy turning of the body. The inner edge of your heels should be about as far apart as the tips of your shoulders. If your feet are too far apart or too close together you'll lose balance as you turn. Turn your right toe out a little bit. That will make it easier for you to get the hip action you need. A common error in addressing the long shots is to have the ball too far to the left. Never have it farther left than in line with the back of the left heel.

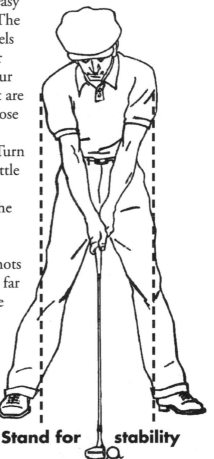

Stand for stability

TIPS ON ADDRESS

I'll give you a few important little tips on getting started correctly to hit the ball: At address, feel that you are slightly "knock-elbowed." With your left arm straight and your right elbow bent and about in line over your right knee, you encourage yourself to swing the club around your shoulder correctly. Straighten your left elbow as you sole the club behind the ball just before starting your swing. If you don't straighten your left arm then you never will get it straight to use as the radius of your swing. Wiggle your toes. That will make sure you're well set on the balls of your feet and your heels.

Elbows close

BODY TURN

Some of the old phrases in golf instruction visualize the desired performance so clearly nobody's been able to beat them. For instance, there is the advice to "twist in the barrel." That means to turn your body during the swing as though you were standing in a barrel. It puts a vivid picture in your mind of winding up for a swing instead of leaning onto your right foot in the backswing then lurching to the left as you try to hit the ball. When you "twist in the barrel" your head stays steady as the hub of your swing and your swing is a swing instead of a series of spasms.

Twist in the barrel

FOOT PLACEMENT

It's a good thing for the average golfer to start his downswing on a full shot by consciously setting his left foot flat on the ground. As he does that he probably simultaneously will begin pulling his straight left arm down and pulling his right elbow close to his ribs. When that action goes on, his head must be kept steady as the center of his turn. Then his right shoulder will come under his chin correctly instead of turning in a flat "roundhouse" swing. When the hands get almost in the same plane as the ball the wrists uncock and whip the clubhead into the ball.

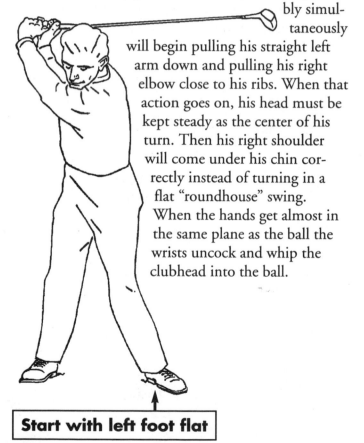

Start with left foot flat

AVOID FORWARD SWAY

"Keep your head behind the ball," as the average golfer should be advised frequently, means that he's got to avoid swaying forward. When he does tilt his center of weight forward as he swings he destroys his aim and slows clubhead speed so the club merely slaps the ball instead of whipping it vigorously.

Set your left foot firmly for your downswing and save your hand action until the latest possible moment, so you can throw the club into the shot instead of throwing yourself. And, above all, you've got to keep your head steady as the hub of your swing.

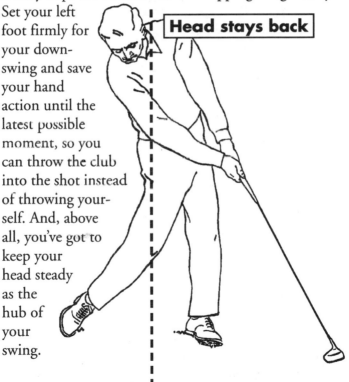

Head stays back

KEEP HEAD STEADY

You've got to keep your head steady or you won't have a center for your swing. I think many typical golfers right at the start get their necks and shoulders so stiff it is impossible for them to swing with any freedom and smoothness. A tip that helps a lot of them is to turn the head a little so the chin points to the right of the ball. Then they can turn their shoulders easily without getting out of balance. They'll find it easier, then, to follow the very old (and still very good) advice to keep the head steady until the left shoulder swings around and under the chin, then until the right shoulder touches the chin. It might give you a simple picture of the swing to think of staying steady while you work your swing from the tip of your left shoulder.

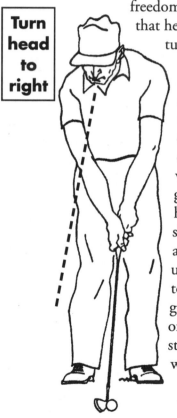

Turn head to right

FREE AND EASY SWING

The ordinary golfer hears "keep your head down" so much that he – or she – starts by holding the chin so close to the chest that there's no possible way of turning the shoulders under the chin and making a free and easy swing. About a 45-degree angle with the ground is the correct head plane for the golfer of normal build. By slightly "sitting down," unlocking your knees, sticking your behind out a trifle and keeping your back fairly upright you get your head in the place where you can swing correctly under your chin.

Chin out

Sit down

FOOT POSITION

The average golfer gets careless about the position of his feet in relation to the ball. Without a sound foundation he hasn't much of a chance to make a decent shot. The ball never should be farther to your left than about a line an inch or so back from your left heel. For a full swing, the inner edges of your feet should be about as far apart as your shoulder tips so you can turn easily and stay in balance. As the length of shot you need gets shorter, your feet should get closer together and your stance should open a bit so you are turned a trifle toward the hole. That's because you don't need body action for the short shots. For the shorter shots, your left foot is toed out to the left a bit and your right foot is about square to the direction line.

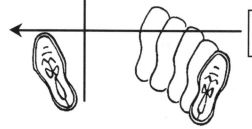

Direction line

Closed stance for drive. Stance opens as shot shortens.

PROPER ADDRESS

Notice how the experts are in a bit of a sitting position as they address the golf ball. This makes sure that their knees are unlocked and they can turn their shoulders and bodies without losing balance. When the golfer's behind is pushed out slightly he's got about as much weight behind the center of the swing as he has in front of it. That protects him against swaying. When he keeps his head steady he can stay behind the plane of the ball in hitting the medium and long shots, and can hit the ball with hand action. When he hits with his hands he plays the shot well; otherwise he throws himself ahead of the ball and hasn't got a chance to hit with any force or precision.

Sit a bit

DON'T REACH

The ordinary golfer is inclined to stand too far away from the ball. Therefore he has to reach for the ball and that invariably puts too much weight on his toes. It also tilts the toe of the club up so he cannot hit with precision or power. At address he should unlock his knees so he is in a slightly sitting position. His weight will be a trifle heavier on his heels. His hands should be close to his legs. The sole of his club should be flat on the ground at address. From this address the club is going to be swung back on a rather upright plane. Then the down-swing is almost certain to be angled down toward the ball. The tendency to try to scoop up the ball therefore will be minimized, if not altogether eliminated.

Hands close to legs

PROTECT AGAINST TENSION

Good, steady balance is attained and retained for the golf swing by protecting yourself against tension. If your muscles are tight you are going to fall out of balance with the first move you make. Set yourself so you never have to stretch for the ball. Usually the closer your hands are to your body the steadier and smoother your swing will be. Ground your club in back of the ball with the sole of the club flat. Then the angle and length of the shaft will show you about how far away from the ball to stand. Never play the ball farther to the left than a line an inch or so to the right of the back of your left heel.

Length and angle of shaft tell you where to stand

HAND POSITION

The only time your hands should be to the right of the plane of the ball at address is when you are addressing a teed-up drive that you will catch on the upswing. Your hands should be ahead of the ball at address for all other shots because you are going to hit those shots on the downswing. The more lofted the club, the farther ahead of the ball your hands should be at address. For the normal 8-iron, 9-iron or pitching wedge shot your left arm and hand and the clubface should be in line with the ball, which should be about even with your right toe.

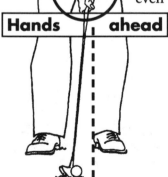

Hands ahead

ELBOW POSITION

Swing the club down to and through the ball on an arc running from inside the direction line of the shot out and across the line. That method is uniformly effective. Golfers who have played baseball visualize this conventional good swing as "hitting toward right field." This swing demands that the right elbow be kept down and rather close to the body, but not cramped. The importance of the right elbow position, which the ordinary golfer rarely realizes, is something the expert heeds the moment he takes his stance at the ball. His right elbow is always easily bent, close to his body and practically in the same vertical plane as his right knee.

Right elbow stays close

TAKE IT EASY

Frequently the average golfer actually fights himself out of making a simple, easy, good shot. He gets stiff and thinks about a lot of details (few of which he understands clearly and can apply deliberately). The first thing he's got to attend to is hitting the ball — a child can do that instinctively, so why complicate the job? Ease and improve your efforts by standing to the ball with your knees and shoulders unlocked; not relaxed to the degree of sagging weakly, but loose enough to allow free motion. Then measure the radius of your swing by positioning the club in back of the ball with your left arm straight.

Loose shoulders

Loose knees

CORRECT ADDRESS

As you address the ball, be sure that your left elbow is straight and your right elbow is a bit bent and close to your body, a little bit forward of, and in line with, your right knee. The orthodox swing of good golf is one that brings the club from inside the direction line out to the ball. It may give you a feeling that you are hitting to the right of your target, but with your left arm straight and your right elbow rather close to your ribs, your clubface will go into the ball square to the direction line and will keep going accurately.

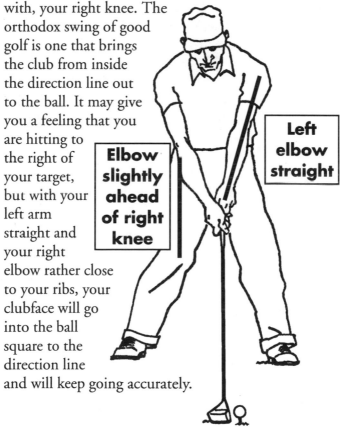

Elbow slightly ahead of right knee

Left elbow straight

HITTING POSTURE

Notice how the experts "sit down" slightly when they address the ball, while ordinary golfers generally stand stiff-kneed. The expert has posture that makes it easy for him to turn his body, keep his head steady and stay in balance. He holds his hands close to his body so he doesn't risk instability and inaccuracy by having to reach for the ball. He pushes his behind out a little, thus establishing a stable center of weight. He can swing smoothly and freely because he unlocks himself as he takes his stance.

Sit down

FOOT FEEL

Winter golf practice will get you in the habit of feeling a good golf swing in your feet. When you address your drive, you should feel that you are firmly flat but not leaden on your feet. When you begin your backswing your weight transfers so you feel that your right leg is the axis of your backswing. At the top of your backswing you are stably set on your right foot and your left heel is a little off the ground. The first thing to do in starting your swing down to the ball is to set your left foot flat on the ground.

Base of the backswing

FIRM LEFT FOOT

The ordinary golfer generally starts his downswing exactly 180 degrees wrong. He should start by settling his left foot firmly on the ground so that almost instinctively there will be a slight push of his left side toward the target. Usually, though, he is in such a mad hurry to get to the ball that he flips his wrists as his first move in bringing the club down. Then there's very little power left when he gets the club to the ball. He should keep his wrists cocked until his hands get about in the same plane as the ball then uncock them swiftly. His left hand must continue to keep moving toward the target.

Downswing starts here

BACKSWING COIL

When you get to the top of a full backswing your right leg is firmly braced and you are quite plainly feeling that your right heel is carrying most of your weight. You're not a bit wobbly as there is a feeling that the ball of your left foot also is a good part of your foundation. When you are coiled this way, your back is almost squarely across the line to the target. Your right leg is tilted toward where you want the shot to go. You should have a feeling that you are wound up and set so you can release a big shot simply by letting your back and arms throw the clubhead around and down and right back up to the point where your wrists uncock and you lash the ball fiercely with your hands.

Brace right foot

STAND UP TO BALL

To hit a golf shot you stand up to the ball; you don't stoop over or squat to reach for it. With your knees unlocked and your behind stuck out just a wee bit you will bend more from your shoulders than from your hips. Your center of balance will run from your shoulders down through the balls of your feet. When you've got yourself properly balanced you will turn in making your swing rather than leaning to the right.

Bend from shoulders

WIGGLE YOUR TOES

As you address the ball you should have the feeling that you are so steady on your feet that you can wiggle your toes inside your shoes. This will protect you against standing so much on your toes that you will fall toward the ball the instant you start the backswing. The ordinary golfer often sways to the right instead of turning early in his backswing. Generally that is because he is standing stiff-kneed. His knees should be unlocked so they will aid rather than impede his body turn.

Steady on your feet

KEEP UNLOCKED

What makes golf difficult is fighting yourself. You tense and get impatient. When you are stiff, tight and move in jerks you haven't got a chance to hit a decent shot. Keep yourself unlocked as you address the ball. Have your knees and shoulders loose but not limp. Instead of thinking about keeping your left arm straight and probably tightening the arm, think only of keeping your left elbow straight. That won't stiffen your arm. Think of swinging the club back with the left arm. That will protect you against a jerky lift with the right hand. Pause at the top of the backswing instead of being impatient to start down.

Loose

Loose

Loose

KNEE POSITION

Notice that expert golfers, when they stand up to make a shot, are slightly knock-kneed and slightly "knock-elbowed," too. By pointing their knees and elbows a little bit inward they put their legs and arms in strong position, yet not tightened. The arms and legs are set so they will work properly in unison. The correct position of the knees at address has the weight a tiny bit heavier on the inner edges of the feet. That gets the expert started by setting up the axis of his backswing on his right leg. It doesn't stiffen his right knee any. He still seems to be "sitting down" a trifle as his hips turn.

Elbows and knees point inward

UNLOCK KNEES

When you address the ball, have your knees unlocked. Stand in a slightly sitting posture and a bit knock-kneed. Standing this way, you can get your knees working so you will turn as much as you need for the shot you want to make. The majority of ordinary golfers are too stiff-legged to get any life into the shot and to stay in good balance. Your knee action in making a golf shot is similar to the way your knees work when you throw a ball underhand.

Sit down a bit

"KNOCK-ELBOW" SWING

As you prepare to make the shot, have your left elbow straight so you almost feel as though you are pressing the clubhead into the ground in back of the ball. Hold your right elbow close to your ribs and practically above your knee. This position, with the elbows close together, sets you in a "knock-elbowed" arrangement that you should maintain throughout the swing. Don't let your left elbow bend or your right elbow fly away from your body and point outward instead of down. If you do, you cannot hit the ball with the uniform left arm radius and the action of the right forearm and hand required for a good shot.

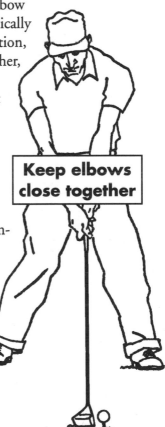

Keep elbows close together

STABLE AXIS

You've got to address the ball so you are set to swing the club around and up, yet still keep your head steady and stay in balance. If your head moves more than just the trifle that's natural to keep you from becoming stiff, you'll lose the stable axis that's absolutely essential to the mechanics of a good swing. Getting based correctly at the start means loosening your knees so you are slightly "sitting down." Have your weight evenly distributed on the balls and heels of your feet. Standing so you feel you're a trifle knock-kneed and your weight is a trifle heavier on the inside edges of your shoes ensures a dependable foundation for your swing.

Sit down

BACKSWING
&
DOWNSWING

PRACTICE FUNDAMENTALS

A certain amount of intelligent experimenting is required in applying the fundamentals of golf. The fundamentals are (1) a grip that holds securely yet allows your hands to wield the club with lively force; (2) an address that sets you so you can swing and hit while you stay in balance; and (3) timing that coordinates every element so you do the right thing at the right time. Your grip should hold the club chiefly with the fingers. Your balance depends on getting set so your head will stay steady as your body turns. Your timing is determined by a smoothly accelerating tempo of the swing culminating in the hitting action of your hands.

Grip

Timing

Stance

FOUR POINTS

Former PGA president and National Open Champion George Sargent said there were four stages in the development of the modern golf swing. The first was about a century ago when young Tom Morris was winning British Open championships by keeping his head steady. Then came Harry Vardon, showing how to stand up and hit the ball with beautiful hand action. The third development was thanks to Bob Jones: the straight but not rigid left arm that established a uniform radius of the swing. Sargent gave me more credit than I think is due me for setting the modern pattern of keeping the right elbow down and fairly close to the ribs so right-side power can be poured into the shot without losing precision.

Hit with hands

Steady head

Straight left arm

Right elbow close

FREE SWING

During the winter the golfer should practice swinging in a manner so free from stiffness that he forgets any other way of making the swing. There are three important points in the free swing. One of them is to keep the left elbow straight. Another is to keep in mind swinging with the left hand and arm in control; the third is to keep the right elbow down and close to the ribs. When you swing this way your wrists are bound to cock at the top of the back-swing if you are holding the club mainly with your fingers as you should be holding it.

Swing relaxed

APPROACH SHOTS

When your approach shots go to the left of the pin your swing may be too flat. You can be certain this is the correct diagnosis if you finish with your hands lower than shoulder level. Two tips that will help you get on the beam: (1) Address the ball with the right elbow close to your ribs and about in line with your right knee, and never let that right elbow fly up or get more than a few inches away from your body. (2) As you take your stance, unlock your knees, stick your rear out a bit and have your chin away from your chest so you can swing your left shoulder under your chin.

Upright swing

PUNCH SHOTS

In the autumn you seldom have much competitive pressure when playing golf, so you can experiment with shots. The punch shot is one to learn. It is very useful for getting out of trouble among trees or when you need an accurate shot into the wind. The punch shot is low and usually stays straight. Generally it's played with a 7-iron, with the stance square, the feet rather close together and the hands ahead of the ball, which is about in line with the right toe. The hands are down on the grip of the club with a couple of inches of the butt end of the club showing. Keep your left arm straight, cock your wrists fairly soon in the back-swing. Take about a half a swing and hit down into the ball. Keep the left hand leading and punch with the right.

Punch down

IRON SHOTS

The typical golfer rarely is much good at a long iron shot (3-, 4- or even 5-iron) primarily because he has not learned that the idea of the stroke is to get the leading edge of the club far enough under the ball so it will be hit squarely by the "sweet spot" of the clubface. That calls for addressing the ball so the hands are above the bottom of the arc of the swing. The ball is almost in the center of the stance — a trifle in back of the line of the left heel. Thus the hands are ahead of the center of the stance. The hands must be comfortably close to the body so the sole of the club is parallel to the ground as the club comes into the ball.

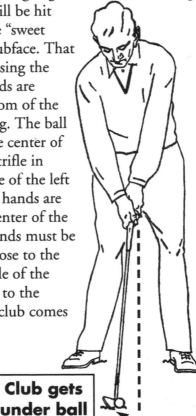

Club gets under ball

ORGANIZE YOUR SHOTS

The good golfer goes at shot-making in an organized way. He thinks of how to hold the club firmly but gently with his fingers, how to stand in relation to the ball and how to swing. The ordinary golfer walks up to the ball and hopes he hits it. No wonder the ordinary golfer grabs the club with a grip that cramps his swing and stands so he is bound to lose his balance when he begins to swing. Then, instead of swinging, he sways over to the right and never turns around to wind up a good swing. The expert golfer stands to the ball so he can swing the club to the top of the back-swing. There he is poised steadily and can take his good time about beginning to swing the club down.

Swing the club up

PROPER SWING

Many fine golfers have a distinct feeling of pulling the club down with the hands almost as if they had the notion of jabbing the butt end of the shaft into the ground. Then when the hands get low in the swing the right hand almost instinctively begins the hit. When the grip is as it should be and your hands are working as a unit, your left hand acts as a guide while your right hand puts the power in. That sensation of your hands pulling down tends to keep your hands comfortably close to your body, directing the path of the clubhead from inside to outside across the projected flight line.

Pull club down

Then HIT!

WIND UP

The reason so many golfers never get very good is that they grab the club with a strong hold from the right hand then lift it away from the ball. They sway instead of winding up for the shot. Anchor the club with the last three fingers of your left hand and place the middle two fingers of your right hand on the grip gently. Then you simply have to swing the club back, around and up "in one piece" with your left arm. When you swing the club with your left hand, arm and shoulder you turn your body properly. Just before you begin your backswing, feel that you are stretching with your left arm so the bend is taken out of your elbow and you've got a steady radius for your swing.

Swing

LIMIT YOUR TIPS

A golf swing can be made up of a million little tips, but never use more than two of them per swing. The ordinary golfer is tip-nutty in trying to find the "secret." To keep him happy, hopeful and minimize his confusion, I tell him to limit his thinking about tips to one tip swinging back and another one swinging into the ball. At the top of the swing when he is changing tips that pause will be good for him. A good tip for going back is to think of his left side and straight left arm swiveling on his right leg (with that knee unlocked). A tip for coming down is to think of getting his right shoulder under his chin. Probably one good tip is all you can apply in action.

Right leg is axis of backswing

MAKING OF AN EXPERT

Here are a few of the major differences between the expert and the ordinary golfer: The expert turns in making his swing; the ordinary golfer leans. The expert hits down at the ball; the ordinary golfer tries to scoop up the shot. The expert stands up, bent a trifle at the knees and shoulders, in addressing the ball and keeps his hands fairly close to his body. The ordinary golfer stands stiffly upright or squats and reaches for the ball. The expert swings the club mainly with his straight left arm; the ordinary golfer lifts the club then sweeps it with his right hand. The expert holds the club principally with his fingers; the ordinary golfer hasn't any idea how he holds it.

Turn

SMOOTH SWING

You should hold the club a little stronger with the last three fingers of the left hand than you hold it with the middle two of the right so you will swing the club back and around from the ball smoothly instead of lifting it with a jerk. That spasmodic lift is almost certain to happen when the right hand grip is accentuated. Another reason for the left hand grip being a bit stronger is so the left arm and hand will guide the club down and through the ball without any weakening or wavering. With the left hand grip correct you will find it simple to place the right hand so it will work in close coordination with the left and get the desired speed into the clubhead.

Watch your finger grip

HASTE MAKES WASTE

Haste certainly makes waste of golf shots. I see many golfers stand at the ball so long they nearly freeze. Then they snatch the club away with a lurch that throws them hopelessly out of balance. Rhythm is an essential of golf. You've got to give yourself enough time for one section of the swing to flow smoothly into the next part of the stroke. Why hurry

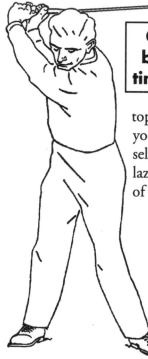

Give your backswing time to finish

to begin your downswing before you finish your backswing? At the top take a look at the ball over your left shoulder and feel yourself in good, easy balance. Be lazy; don't make hard, fast work of a golf shot or you'll ruin it.

SMOOTH BACKSWING

When you begin your backswing smoothly you probably will be OK the rest of the way. It's the jerky start, the lift of the club with the right hand and a sway to the right that ruin the swing of the ordinary golfer. A good exercise to get yourself in the habit of swinging correctly is to practice with only the left hand holding the club. Then swing the club keeping your left arm straight. Swing the club back over your right shoulder and let the wrists cock themselves at the top. Then pull the club down with the wrists still cocked. The left arm is for swinging and steering the club. The right arm and hand are for hitting.

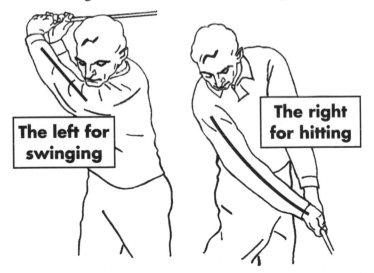

The left for swinging

The right for hitting

DON'T HURRY SWING

Your practice swing usually is much better than the swing you take at the ball because you don't rush the practice swing. When you start smoothly and without a jerk you give yourself enough time to get clear to the top of your backswing. Then you instinctively pause there until you get fully arranged to swing the club down to the ball. With this pause you save

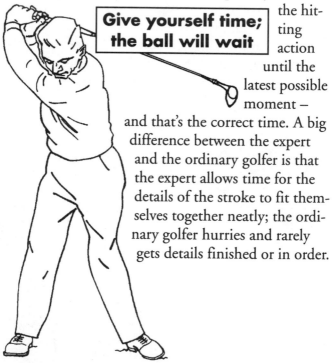

Give yourself time; the ball will wait

the hitting action until the latest possible moment – and that's the correct time. A big difference between the expert and the ordinary golfer is that the expert allows time for the details of the stroke to fit themselves together neatly; the ordinary golfer hurries and rarely gets details finished or in order.

CALL A HALT

When your swing has fallen apart and you need help right now, pause an instant at the top of your swing. That's often the magic moment when you can "get well." During that brief, almost imperceptible halt, you instinctively arrange yourself so that you (1) Get into steady balance; (2) Firm your grip with the last three fingers of the left hand; (3) Get your right elbow down and fairly close to your ribs; and (4) Set your left foot flat on the ground so you are ready to start your downswing.

PAUSE at the checkpoint

SWING CONTROL

To complete your backswing for a long shot you've got to cock your wrists fully. That means the club shaft has to be at a right angle to your straight left arm; maybe even a bit past that point if you still can keep it under control. At the top of the backswing and everywhere else during the swing, control comes from having the last three fingers of your left hand securing the club against the heel of your hand. Control also calls for having your left thumb under the shaft at the top of the backswing so the thumb will help support the club. With this sort of left-hand connection you can get a big arc for your swing.

Cock wrists fully at top

UNHURRIED SWING

When your swing is unhurried, giving you a fraction-of-a-second pause at the top of the backswing, you won't have much trouble hitting a golf ball well. It is the rushing swing that jerks a golfer off balance. It's that frantic speed that has him starting down before he really is steadily set at the top of the swing and is "drawing a bead" on the ball over his left shoulder. It is the spasmodic swing and not the swing in smooth rhythm that tears the stroke to pieces. Perhaps your natural tempo is swift; maybe it's lazy, but however it's paced, it is right for golf if it allows you to pause at the top of the backswing.

WAIT!

PROPER TIMING

The average golfer seldom gets a good long shot because he seldom has proper timing. He gets impatient and jerks the club swiftly away from the ball with an effort that destroys balance at the start of the backswing. Then after getting to the farthest point of the backswing the ordinary golfer erroneously starts the downswing by uncocking the wrists. Keep the wrists cocked and the right angle of the left arm and clubshaft as long as you possibly can in the downswing. When you have good timing your hands will be about in line with the ball before your wrists uncock and you lash the club into the shot.

Wrists uncock here →

STAY IN BALANCE

If you can teach yourself to stay in balance as you swing, your winter golf practice will immensely improve your game. The majority of ordinary golfers throw themselves, instead of their hands and the club, at the ball because they don't establish a center around which they can swing. Notice from these illustrations how the center of weight provides an axis from which the club is whipped around into the ball. Remember that, as a general thing, you swing with your left arm and hit with your right forearm and hand. You have got to have a steady center for that performance.

Center of swing

STABLE SWING

The post-mortem of your bad shot offered by a 100-shooting playing companion probably blames you for "lifting your head." But 9 times out of 10, raising your head is an effect rather than the primary cause of a bad shot. It generally indicates stiff

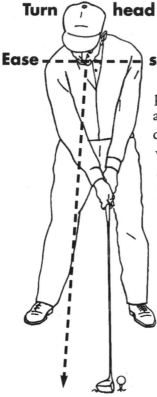

Turn head

Ease shoulders

and unstable posture and stance at address. Turn your head a bit to the right so your nose points to the right of the ball and that'll allow your shoulders to turn easily. Stand with your back, from hips to shoulders, fairly erect and your knees bent so you are somewhat "sitting down." Do not reach out for the ball. Then you can swing in stable balance without jerking your head up.

ADDRESSING THE BALL

Think of having your left elbow straight as you address the ball and swing the club, rather than thinking about keeping your left arm straight to establish and maintain the radius of the swing. When you think only of the left elbow there is less tendency to stiffen, slow down and cramp your action than when you try to keep your left arm straight as a rod. Many of the shots topped by ordinary golfers are the result of bending the elbow rather than lifting the head. Get in the habit of soling the club behind the ball and that will remind you to straighten your left elbow.

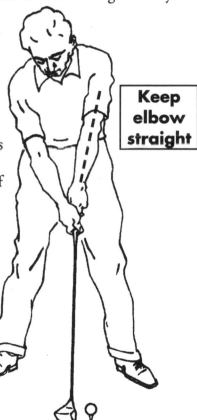

Keep elbow straight

STAY IN BALANCE

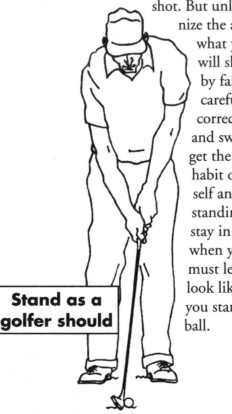

Stand as a golfer should

Carelessness accounts for a great many bad shots by the ordinary golfer. Through these lessons you have been getting from me, you now should know the simple things that must be done to make a good golf shot. But unless you organize the application of what you know you will slop away shots by failing to make a careful routine of correct grip, stance and swing. You must get the intelligent habit of aiming yourself and your club and standing so you will stay in sound balance when you swing. You must learn how to look like a golfer as you stand up to the ball.

RIGHT KNEE PUSH

Watch how every good golfer gets his right foot and leg into every shot of moderate or considerable length. At the start of the downswing the left foot is firmly set on the ground and the left leg becomes the axis of the swing. The right knee pushes into the shot. From the ball of the right foot there is springing action, moving the body and arms into position for the hit. If your right leg is stuck and stiff you haven't got a chance of making a shot that's got a lot of power in it. Get your right knee working as it would if you were throwing a ball underhand and you'll probably add a good many yards to your shots.

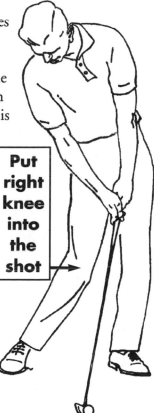

Put right knee into the shot

STAY DOWN

Many a time I have found that the way to get a golfer hitting the ball well is by giving him a vivid mental picture of what must be done. Then he is able to work out the right answer his own way. The imaginative treatment was old stuff in golf instruction before I was born, but it is still helpful. It accents learning rather than teaching. For instance, when a pupil was "coming off the ball" – meaning he was not staying down and keeping his left arm straight until the shot was finished – old masters of instruction used to advise: "Imagine there are three balls close together on the line to the hole. Then pretend you are going to hit all three of them. That way you'll certainly stay down until the ball is correctly on its way."

Keep hitting

HIT HARD

The majority of golfers don't play their long iron shots well for the simple reason that they hold back in playing these clubs. To hit a long iron, place your right foot a trifle farther away than your left foot from the direction line. This closed stance will enable you to get more of a body turn. Play the ball a little ahead of the center of your stance. Take a big, unhurried backswing, pause an instant at the top, then pull the club down with your straight left arm and whip it into the ball as viciously as you can. You can't possibly hit a good, long iron shot by playing it gently.

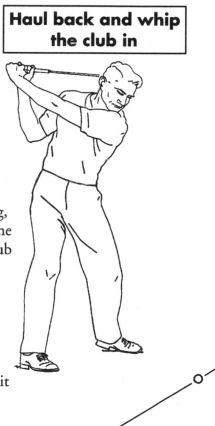

Haul back and whip the club in

Simple Swing

So many players make the mistake of thinking that the golf swing is extremely complicated. Actually, the simpler you can visualize and make the swing the better it is. Merely turn and swing your straight left arm around and up while keeping your right elbow down and close to your ribs. Then, in coming down, don't think about sliding the left hip to "get it out of the way," but get your entire right side into the shot in the same manner you'd throw a ball under-hand. That will bring your shoulders about parallel to the direction line as you reach the place and time for hitting the ball.

Throw it underhand

GOOD IRON PLAY

The ordinary golfer, if he does practice, practices with his wood clubs more than with his irons, yet his irons are the most constructive part of his game. Once he learns to play good iron shots, the teed-up drives and the fairway wood shots are easy. In making the long iron shots, think of swinging your left hand up and around so the shaft will come across your left shoulder about halfway between the tip of the shoulder and the neck. Then pull the club down with your left hand and whip it through the shot with your right. On the short iron shots remember to keep your weight on your left foot throughout the swing.

Pull with left then whip with right

MAKING THE SHOT

In making a good golf shot you swing the club with your left side and hit with your right. That's over-simplifying the procedure, but the description may clarify your moving picture of what you've got to do — and how to do it. Your left hand holds the club firmly, your left arm is straight, your left knee turns and points to the right of the ball and your left shoulder touches your chin as you swing the club back. When

Swing with the left side

Hit with the right side

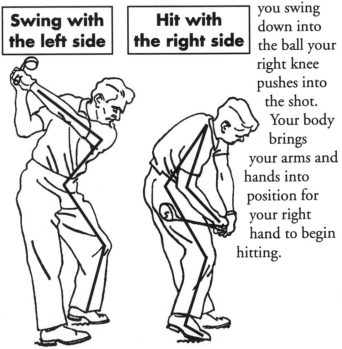

you swing down into the ball your right knee pushes into the shot. Your body brings your arms and hands into position for your right hand to begin hitting.

HIT DOWN

You've got to hit down on all your shots except the putts and the teed-up drive, which can be hit on the upswing. That means you've got to hit down and get underneath the ball with the sole of the club. Hence you must keep your left elbow straight, and with the hands pull the lower part of the club-face beneath the ball into the position where the right hand puts power into the shot. The left hand functions as the guide. While you are swinging, the right elbow must stay down and close to your ribs. Delay uncocking your wrists as long as you can to put a swift, firm whip into the shot.

Hitting hand

Guiding hand

DOWNSWING FEEL

It is good to have the feeling in your downswing that you are vigorously pulling your left hand down toward the ball. This sensation helps you keep your left arm straight and preserve the radius of the swing. This pulling also has a tendency to keep the last three fingers of the left hand in secure control of the club and delay the right-hand hitting action until the correct moment. You should maintain the 90-degree angle between the left arm and the club shaft until the last possible moment.

Pull left hand towards ball

STAY BACK OF BALL

The expert golfer looks almost like he is falling away from the ball, from his hips up, as he hits. The average golfer often does the opposite. He leans toward the target as he hits what he hopes will be a long shot – but isn't. The steady head position of the expert as he throws the club out after the ball accounts for what is called "staying back of the ball." The ordinary golfer will find it easier to stay behind the ball if he keeps his head steady until his right shoulder touches his chin. If you're the fellow who is trying to keep his head steady, avoid the error of getting stiff-necked. That will cramp your shoulder movement.

Stay steady back of the ball

DON'T QUIT ON A SHOT

One big difference between the expert golfer and the ordinary player is that the expert never quits on a shot. His left arm and hand continue to lead toward the target. His right leg continues to push so it swings his body around in a power performance perfectly coordinated with the hand action. The power comes from the right side: the back muscles, forearm

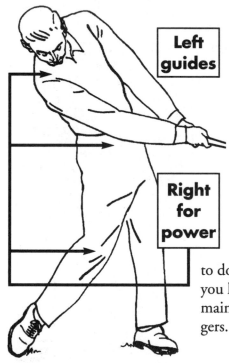

Left guides

Right for power

and leg. The direction is guided by the left side and arm. Keep your left arm moving throught the shot and your right knee moving into it and you will hit the ball well. Of course, you've got to have a firm and flexible grip to do this. That means you hold the club mainly with your fingers.

SWINGING HIT

The golf stroke is a swinging hit. You swing the club back with your arms, and the centrifugal force that induces cocking your wrists (if your grip is correct) will add more distance to your swing and your shot. Then, keeping your wrists cocked so the shaft is at about a right angle with your left arm, you continue to swing down toward the ball. With the left arm as the main guiding element and the right elbow down and close to the ribs, your hands get in line with the ball. Then the hit begins. Hit fiercely with your right hand but never let the left hand or arm weaken.

Keep wrists cocked

STAND STEADY

The expert golfer throws the club at the ball; the ordinary golfer nearly throws himself at it. When making a golf shot you've got to stand steady, turn on a stable axis, swing with your arms and hit with your hands as the clubhead accelerates into the ball. This steadiness depends on keeping your head still but not to the degree that your neck is stiff. Turn your head a trifle to the right as you address the shot. This will help you get free shoulder action. Practice so you can watch the shadow of your head stay steady.

Head stays steady

Club is thrown

HAND ACTION

The reason so many ordinary golfers never finish a shot is that they let go with the left hand. You've got to keep the tips of the last three fingers of your left hand securing the club against the heel of that hand or you lose control of the club. When that happens, the right hand, instead of applying power to the shot the correct way, turns over the left hand in a weak way. The steady grip of the last three fingers of the left hand is the fulcrum for the effective leverage of hand action in a good golf shot.

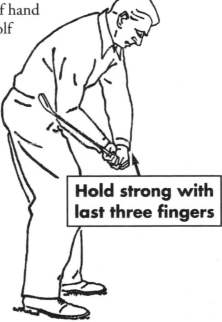

Hold strong with last three fingers

GET RIGHT SIDE IN

My sympathy is with the average golfer who is exposed to such confusing advice as "get the left side out of the way." It means, I suspect, that you should not cramp your shot. But doesn't it make better sense to be told to put your right side *into* the shot? Then your muscles realize that you must have your right knee unlocked so it will naturally go to the left as you are coming into the ball. That way, your whole right side will move just about as it would if you were throwing a ball underhand. Whatever your right side does in a positive way is going to have your left side functioning in coordination. When you get a chance to see Arnold Palmer play, watch how he gets his right knee into shots. He doesn't get the left side out, he gets the right side in.

Put right side into the shot

HIT DOWN

Golf's experts hit down at every shot except the teed-up drive, which is caught on the upswing. The club on a downswing "pops" the ball on its way. The club is made to do that, but the ordinary golfer wants to scoop the ball up. That's why he misplays so many shots. You can see the difference when a really good golfer hits an iron or fairway wood shot. If his hands, at address, are in front of the plane of the ball, he is sure to hit the ball before the club reaches the bottom of its arc. The tendency of the common golfer is to have the ball too far to the left at address so there isn't a chance in the world to hit it with a good, vigorous, accurate blow. Unless the average golfer is careful the ball seems to creep to the left, and whenever it gets farther than the line off the back of the left heel it cannot be hit well.

Clubface hits the ball up

AIM AT SPOT

If you are the typical golfer, you hope for a good shot instead of thinking. The instant you step up to the ball you get engulfed in a fog instead of seeing distinctly a spot on the back of the ball against which you know you've got to smack the clubface accurately to get the shot that you want. Forget that generality about looking at the ball. Look at that one place on the ball where you want to apply the club. Then ease yourself so you can naturally and easily swing around and up and down and whip the club at the spot where you are aiming. It is amazing how much your instinct will help you when you keep yourself from getting tight.

Pinpoint your aim

FINISHING A SHOT

Notice how the experts finish a full shot with their hands high over their heads. They can't help getting that fine finish. They have done the right thing and haven't quit on the shot. They have got themselves set so they can hit with the hands. That means throwing the club out after the ball and allowing the hands to finish high. It also means staying down to the ball until the right shoulder touches the chin. Allowing the right arm to straighten after the ball is hit is almost as important as keeping the left arm straight in swinging to the ball.

Throw your hands

TWO MISTAKES

The golfer who fails to improve generally has two serious mistakes in his stance. He plays the ball so far ahead of the line with the back of his left heel that he does not give himself a chance to hit the ball on the downswing or at the very bottom of the swing arc, as all good shots (except the teed-up drive) must be hit. He also makes the error of reaching for the ball, and either falls out of balance or hits the ball feebly with the toe of the club – if he connects. Get in the habit of soling the club, squarely aimed, in back of the ball and let the angle and length of the club shaft dictate where you should stand.

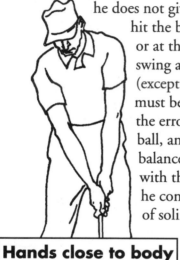

Hands close to body

Hit the ball at the lowest point of swing

SIDEHILL LIES

Sidehill lies frequently are very well played by the ordinary golfer because he gets careful and thinks. He knows he must stay in good balance and hit with his hands instead of falling into or away from the shot. Consequently he sets himself solidly so he can swing his arms without much body turning. That means his weight is going to be mainly on his left foot whether the lie is uphill or downhill. When you face the ball and it is uphill from your feet, hold the club a little shorter and aim to the right as you probably will hook the shot. When the ball is lying below your feet, bend your knees and sit down a wee bit more than usual to the shot.

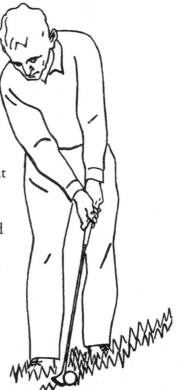

LONG SHOTS

To make a long golf shot you've got to finish high. Of course, you don't hit the ball with your follow-through, but what happens before you hit the ball and as you hit it will show in your finish. The usual reason the ordinary golfer does not have a good natural follow-through is that he is out of balance as he swings, and consequently he actually stops hitting hard before he even hits the ball. Get a firm but not frozen grip, keep your head steady and have the feeling you are going to hit with a fierce whip of your right hand. Then you're pretty sure to finish the shot correctly.

Finish high

LONG LEFT THUMB

Every time I've have a student patient enough for intelligent research on the grip, I've had a man or woman who became a much-better-than-average golfer. To some degree the grip is as individual as penmanship, but whatever the grip's delicate variations might be, they've got to allow the club to work easily and stay under control. Remember that the club is used flexibly like a whip, not stiffly like an ax. Something that helps most golfers (but not all the experts) is what's called the "long left thumb." Stretched along the top backside of the shaft, with the butt of the right thumb snugly over it, it will help support the club at the top of the backswing.

Hold club like a whip

LOOK IN MIRROR

You can get yourself into the habit of looking like a golfer by inspecting your address in a full-length mirror. Note your foot and hand positions in relation to the ball. The ball never should be farther to the left than a line an inch or so back from the left heel. The feet are about shoulder-width apart for the long shots; closer together as the shots get shorter. When the sole of the club is flat on the ground directly in back of the ball the length and angle of the shaft determine the distance you should stand from the ball. Your posture is comfortably upright with your knees bent a little and your behind pushed out a trifle.

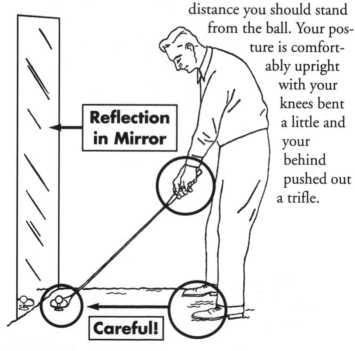

Reflection in Mirror

Careful!

RIGHT HAND GRIP

Neglect of apparently simple little things will ruin a golf shot. For instance: If you hold the club too tightly with the thumb and forefinger of your right hand you are sure to restrict action of the club-head when you need it, forcing your right shoulder to fly out and around too high instead of under your chin. The instant I see a golfer spasmodically grab with his right hand as he starts to swing, I want to yell, "Please don't!" I know what's coming.

Shoulder under the chin

His right hand going into command too early will freeze his right side and collapse his left arm.

STEADY HEAD

Notice how the expert golfer seems to bend away from the direction of his strong shot as he connects with the ball. This is because his head is staying steady and his right leg has moved his body around into position for the hit. The head is the hub of the axle of your swing. When the head moves to the left you slow the speed of the clubhead and change its position so you cannot possibly make a satisfactory shot.

The head is the hub of the swing

THE
SHORT
GAME

A Putting Secret

If there is any secret to good putting, I see it exhibited on winter vacations by people who play golf enjoyably but without knowing much about the game. They go at putting as though it were easy and nothing to worry about. So, instinctively they keep their heads steady and have a smooth, slow stroke because that's the only simple way of keeping the face of the putter moving squarely on the line to the hole.

To these people, hitting the ball hard is a difficult job but rolling it easily over a smooth green into the hole is not. If I didn't know putting was as nervously uncertain as I can make it, I'd be beating the best of them. Pretend-putting is easy — I wish I could do it.

Simply ⟶ ‑Ọ putting ➔ ⬭

PICTURE A PUTT

About all there is to putting is to keep your head steady and the face of your putter square to the direction line as you stroke the ball. The "touch" (which means estimating the power required for the length of the putt) comes almost instinctively when you get a clear mental picture of the putt and keep your head still. There are millions of grips, stances and postures for individual golfers. You can learn by home practice the ones that suit you. Putt on your carpet at a glass or a chair leg and stretch a thread on the floor by your ball so you will get in the habit of studying exactly how your putter moves. Another thing to watch for is the place on the face of your putter that is the "sweet spot," which the ball must contact to move accurately.

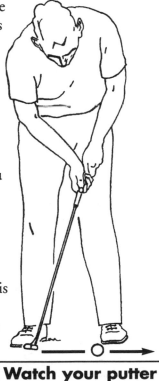

Watch your putter

PRACTICE PUTTING

You ought to work out a system for your putting. You can do this in putting practice at home. The majority of average golfers haven't even a studied method of holding the putter. They hold it either too tightly or so weakly that there's no decisiveness about the stroke. Usually the weakness is that they have failed to have the tips of the last two or three fingers of the left hand firmly – but not stiffly – holding the club. The left hand is important in steering the putter. The sensitive forefinger and thumb touch of the right hand grip supplies, instinctively, the feel of the distance required for the putt.

Steering

The 'touch'

PUTTING TIPS

Maybe you've noticed that there are more putts to the left of the cup than to the right. The simple explanation is that the left wrist collapses and bends in while the right hand takes command of the putt. Then the right hand rolls over the left and a hooked putt results. Another common error of the typical golfer is that of stroking the ball too near the toe of the putter. That exaggerates the tendency to curl the putt to the left. The "wristier" the putt is, the more chance there is for error. You also may have a lot more confidence in your putts when you learn where the "sweet spot" is on your putter – the spot on the putter face that sends the putts rolling straight.

Keep left wrist straight

MORE PUTTING TIPS

All players who putt well do two things: (1) They keep the head absolutely steady, and (2) They bring the face of the putter to the ball precisely square to the line of the putt. Those two things Bob Jones, Walter Hagen, Gene Sarazen, Ben Hogan and others and I did when we were winning the Big Ones. Palmer, Nicklaus and other stars share the same two essentials. There are countless individual ways of doing these two things. Arnold Palmer's knock-kneed putting stance is his own way of keeping his head steady. Maybe it's also your best way. Maybe it isn't. You'll have to find out by studious experimenting and practicing. Plan and conduct your putting practice to intelligently test some detail of your method instead of merely patting golf balls toward a hole.

Head steady

Putter face square

PENDULUM SWING

When your putting goes sour (and whose doesn't?), try a pendulum swing from your shoulders. This will cure you if you have been too wristy and rolling your right hand over your left. Try having your left hand mainly underneath the club grip. Pick a spot a few inches ahead of the ball on the line of the putt and watch until your putter moves squarely across that line. That will help keep your head steady and the face of the putter square to the line. Stand so your eyes are over the ball. That may protect you against stroking the ball too near the toe of the putter.

Swing from shoulders

PUTTING CURES

When your putting is off, begin the cure by making sure that your eyes are over the ball as you putt and your head stays absolutely dead steady. This

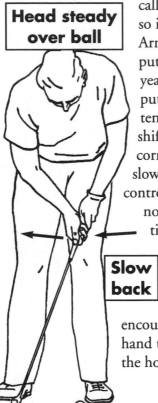

Head steady over ball

Slow back

calls for setting your weight so it won't shift readily. Arnold Palmer was the best putter I'd seen in many years. His knock-kneed putting stance checks any tendency he might have to shift his weight. Another correction is to go back very slowly with your left hand in control so the clubface does not get outside the direction line. Something else to make your putting get well is to get a grip that won't let your wrists roll over but will encourage the back of your left hand to move squarely toward the hole.

FORGET COMPLICATIONS

The average golfer is confused enough when he gets up to putt without trying to remember all he's read and heard about reading greens. All he needs to think about is getting the ball into the hole by rolling it along what looks to be the correct line. He should forget the complications and delicate little details (which he probably couldn't perform anyway). Let him keep his head absolutely steady and move his putter face so it meets the ball at a right angle to the direction line, relying on what his eyes tell his senses of touch and direction to take care of the slopes and speed of the green.

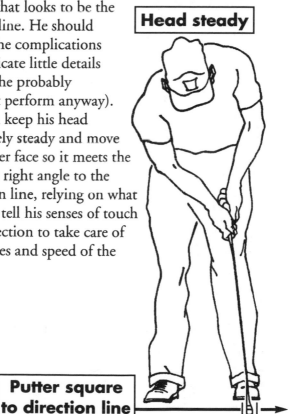

Head steady

Putter square to direction line

PUTTER AIM

Put your palms together in front of you in a prayerful position and you get the idea of how the back of your left hand and the palm of your right hand should work together to keep the face of your putter squarely across the direction line. This precision must be maintained during the backswing and the follow-through. The consistently good putters move their feet, not their hands, forearms or shoulders to achieve the correct direction of the stroke. You've got to keep your head steady or you risk turning your shoulders just enough to angle the face of the putter away from an accurate pendulum swing. Practice your short putts first and they will teach you how to take and maintain precise aim with your putter face.

Hands and putter face work together

PRECISION SHOTS

Two things you should study about the way experts play short and medium shots: (1) The way they "sit down" a little bit as they address the ball, and (2) The way they keep their hands close to the body at address. These actions enable them to keep the body steadily balanced without the slightest degree of stiffness.

The hands stay close to the body during the swing. The shots that require precision rather than power are played primarily by swinging the arms; then, just about the time the hands get even with the ball, uncocking the wrists and slapping the club into the shot. There's very little body action required; just enough to allow the swing to be smooth.

Hands close to body

KNOW YOUR PUTTER

Many golfers never get to know their putters. You will see them with the sole of the putter not flat on the ground as they sole it behind the ball. That means one of two things: They are handicapping themselves either by having a putter that lies too flat or upright to be used with consistent precision, or by not maintaining a correct stance at the putt. These uncertain putters also haven't located the "sweet spot" on the face of the putter, where the club is balanced and from which the ball will roll without deviation along the line of aim. If the ball is putted from a spot too much toward the toe of the putter it will have a counter-clockwise spin that will roll the putt off the line. A center-shafted putter has its "sweet spot" about in line with where the shaft is joined to the putter head.

Find the 'sweet spot'

IMPROVING THE SHORT GAME

Feel that your elbows are being brought together instead of being sloppily spread apart. Feel that your left arm is straight. Then you are sure to improve your short game. Hold the club firmly with the last three fingertips of the left hand pushing it against the lower part of the palm of your hand. And by all means have the fingers of your right hand on the club so the nearest third of your right index finger is against the part of the grip that is away from the hole and the tip of that finger is gently securing the club. Then swing from your left shoulder.

Keep elbows from spreading

SHORT SHOTS

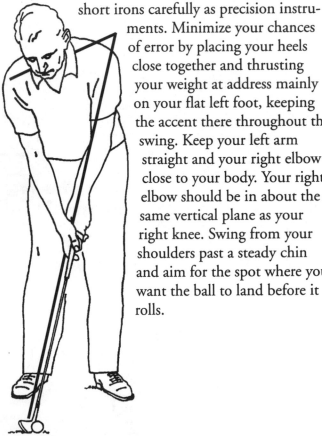

At 50 yards away from the cup, the expert often holes out in two strokes. The ordinary player usually needs four strokes because he doesn't use the short irons carefully as precision instruments. Minimize your chances of error by placing your heels close together and thrusting your weight at address mainly on your flat left foot, keeping the accent there throughout the swing. Keep your left arm straight and your right elbow close to your body. Your right elbow should be in about the same vertical plane as your right knee. Swing from your shoulders past a steady chin and aim for the spot where you want the ball to land before it rolls.

MORE SHORT SHOTS

Just one little bit of advice will prevent a lot of headaches for you on short shots: Keep your left arm straight from your knuckles to your shoulder – and swing it toward the hole. Often the ordinary golfer lets his left elbow and wrist buckle and flips his right hand into the shot. That's fatal. Keep the hands moving toward the hole. That's easily done when you think of maintaining a straight line from your left shoulder through the shaft of your club as you hit those short shots and as you follow through. Keep your right shoulder swinging under the chin, which you have held steady.

Keep left arm straight and swinging

PITCH SHOTS

Often the pitch shots of average golfers fall short for the simple reason that the player forgets to swing the lofted club back far enough. The trajectory of the shot calls for more power than generally is given to these high, short pitches. That is why so many of them fall into traps that should have been easily carried. Keep the left arm straight and swing the club back until the left shoulder comes under the chin. Keep your head steady and swing down at the ball with the left arm straight. Get the leading edge of the club swinging beneath the ball and the loft of the club will lift the ball as you are hitting down.

Swing shoulder under chin

CHIP SHOTS

When you are playing a short chip or pitch shot be very careful to have your left shoulder working. Swing the club from your left shoulder with your left arm straight and your right elbow down and close to your ribs. The cocking of your wrists is a secondary action, but the average golfer often attempts his short approach shots with a jerky, "wristy" action that either tops the ball or chops into the turf behind it. When you are making a long pitch shot, swing your arms back plenty because the high trajectory of the shot with a lofted club will kill distance.

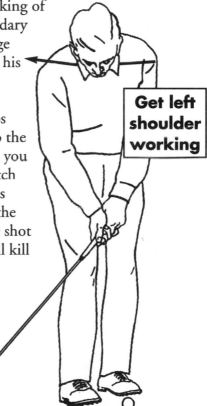

Get left shoulder working

SHORT SHOTS

When you address short shots – pitches or chips – have your weight accented on your left foot and keep it there all through the swing. You should make this swing with your straight left arm as the major lever. Your shoulder turn is about all the turn you need. Your body moves just enough to protect you against being tight and jerky. Have your hands ahead of the ball at address and the club shaft about in line with your left arm. Keep your right elbow close to your ribs and in the same plane as your right knee. Then it is easy to hit down properly on the ball.

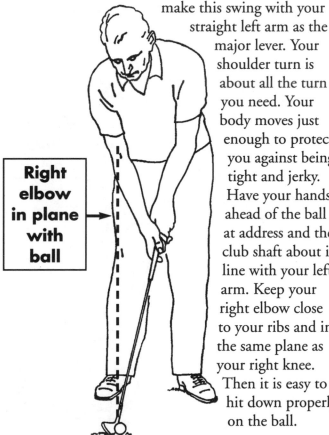

Right elbow in plane with ball

FOOT WORK

The shorter the shot, the closer together your feet are at address. That is because you do not need much body action for the short shots. Just turn your shoulders, swing your arms and whip your hands into the strokes that call for precision without power. For the long shots, stand with the insides of your heels about as far apart as your shoulder tips; then you can stay steady as you turn. The shorter the shot, the farther your hands are in front of the ball at address, so you will hit down and get the bottom edge of the club under the ball instead of trying to scoop it up. Never have the ball at address ahead of a line an inch or so to the right of your left heel.

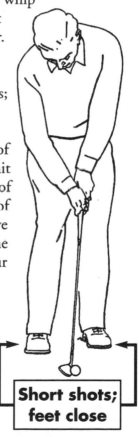

Short shots; feet close

PITCH SHOTS

Pitch shots from about 20 to 80 yards from the hole should finish close enough to give you a good chance to sink your putt. For precision, you play those shots with very little body action. Stand slightly facing the hole with your heels only a few inches apart and your right foot at a right angle to the direction line. Play the ball about in line with your right toe. Keep your weight accented on your left foot at address and all through the shot. Your left arm has got to stay straight and your right elbow close to your ribs. The swing is a shoulder-and-hand performance.

Open stance

APPROACH SHOTS

The average golfer misplays many of his short approach shots because he is too "wristy." He usually can cure himself of excessive cocking of his wrists by simply swinging the club back with his left elbow straight – with a feeling of firmly holding the club with the **Swing easy** last three fingers of his left hand. When he gets this short and unhurried backswing started with his left hand and arm in control, keeping his head steady, he won't top the approach. What usually ruins his shot is snatching the club up by cocking his wrists in starting his backswing.

SHORT APPROACHES

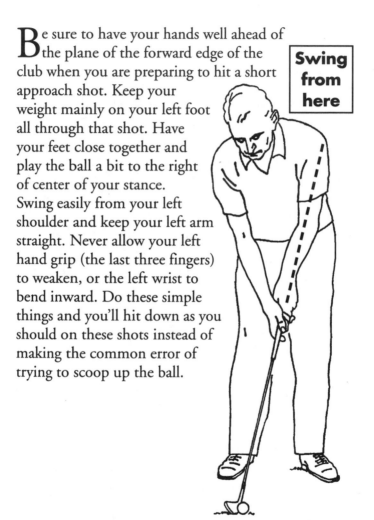

Swing from here

Be sure to have your hands well ahead of the plane of the forward edge of the club when you are preparing to hit a short approach shot. Keep your weight mainly on your left foot all through that shot. Have your feet close together and play the ball a bit to the right of center of your stance. Swing easily from your left shoulder and keep your left arm straight. Never allow your left hand grip (the last three fingers) to weaken, or the left wrist to bend inward. Do these simple things and you'll hit down as you should on these shots instead of making the common error of trying to scoop up the ball.

WEDGE SHOTS

Confidence is a big factor in playing a wedge shot well out of a sand trap onto an adjoining green. It is a simple shot. Really, the wedge's flange makes it easier for you to make the shot from a normal lie in the sand than to miss it.

First, get a firm footing in the sand so your stance is open and the ball is to the left of the center of your stance. Keep your weight mainly on your left foot. You need very little body turn. Keep your left arm stretched all through the shot. Cock your wrists early in the backswing. Keep your right elbow down and close to your ribs. Hit into the sand about $1\frac{1}{2}$ inches behind the ball and follow through, head steady. Never quit on the shot.

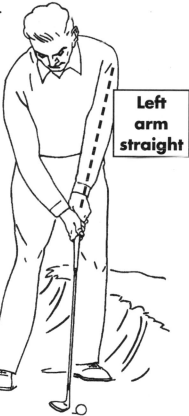

Left arm straight

PRECISION SHOTS

Address your medium and short shots with your weight slightly heavier on your left foot. You need very little body turn in making these shots. A little shoulder turning, swinging your arms and hitting with your hands, is all you need for these precision shots. You've got to swing down so the ball is hit just before the club gets to the bottom of the arc of the swing. That's the reason for having your weight a bit to the left. It is the reason, too, for having the ball to the right of the center of your stance and your hands ahead of the ball at address.

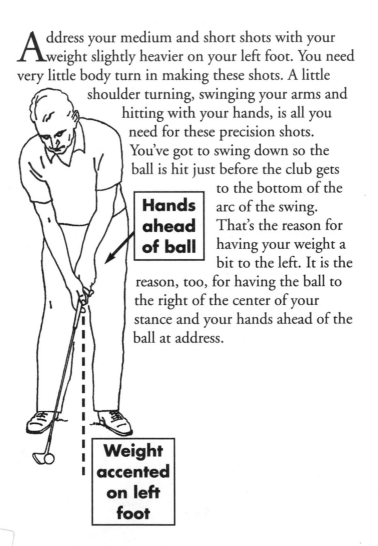

Hands ahead of ball

Weight accented on left foot

SHORT CHIPS

The most exasperating shot in golf is the short chip or pitch that is misplayed when a "wristy" chop with the club either digs it into the ground in back of the ball or tops the shot. To play this shot correctly keep your weight chiefly on your left leg. Your head has got to stay still. Swing the club with your left elbow straight. Swing the club from your left shoulder and swing it back smoothly. Why hurry? You can hold the club a bit firmer with the fingers than your grip for

Swing from your left shoulder

long shots because you don't need wrist action on the short shots. Control the club with pressure from the last three fingers of your left hand.

CHIP SHOTS

Good chip shots are practically elongated putts that light on the green and roll toward the hole. To make them it is essential to keep your head dead steady as if you were putting. Hold the club low on

Head steady

the grip, with a little firmer finger grip than you'd have for longer shots. Have your hands working as one so you can swing the back of the left hand back and forth along the direction line. Break the wrists a little in making the

Left wrist firm

shot, but be sure your left wrist doesn't bend so the clubface gets ahead of alignment with the left arm as you stroke the ball.

OFF-GREEN SHOTS

The expert, when he is 15 to 25 yards off the green, expects to get the ball close enough to the hole to get down in one putt. The ordinary golfer is lucky if, from the same range, he gets within 6 feet of the cup. The difference is explained by the fact that the expert holds the club near the bottom of the grip. He keeps his weight mainly on his left foot and plays the ball far enough back from the center of his stance to be sure he swings down at the ball and doesn't try to scoop it up. The expert also holds the club mainly with the left hand and keeps the back of that hand going toward the hole instead of allowing the right hand to roll over the left.

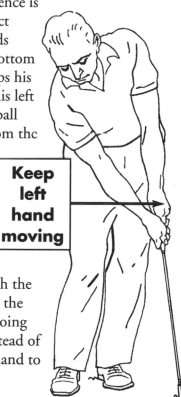

Keep left hand moving

HANDS CLOSE TO BODY

Stand to the ball so you can make the shot easily. For instance: On those short pitches that are made with your shoulders, arms and hands with practically no body movement, stand with your right foot at a right angle to the direction line and your left foot pointed slightly toward the hole so you will swing the club straight back or even a bit outside the line. Your hands are close to your body and ahead of the ball at address. Your heels are just a little bit apart and you are in a sitting posture so there's no tendency to tighten up. Keep your left arm straight and your right elbow about in line with your right knee.

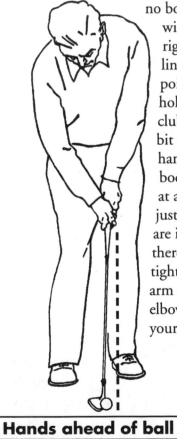

Hands ahead of ball

WEDGE SHOTS

Imagine playing a wedge shot out of a sand trap with a kitchen spoon as big as your wedge – then you'll have the right mental picture of how the wedge should be used to splash a ball out of sand onto a green. You would hold your left arm straight so you wouldn't change the distance between yourself and the ball. Then you would cock your wrists soon after you started to swing away from the ball. You would keep your head steady and swing your arms with just enough body turn to keep you from feeling stiff. You'd pull the spoon down into the sand in back of the ball, under it and up into the air so the sand in your imaginary spoon would bring the ball out with it. The wedge shot out of sand is golf's easiest shot for the fellow who isn't scared of it.

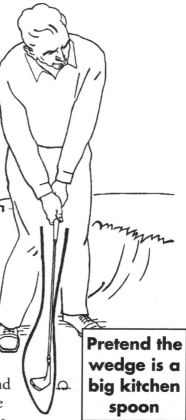

Pretend the wedge is a big kitchen spoon

A GOOD BUNKER SHOT

Do a few simple things right and a good golf shot is bound to happen. The drawing here was made from a successful bunker shot a great player made at a critical time. Notice the few essentials that made the satisfactory result inevitable: The head is steady while the right shoulder comes against the chin. Both arms are straight. The hands are moving well ahead of the ball – they didn't stop when the wedge hit into the sand. The knee is getting into the shot. The left hand is steering the club while the right hand whips the club under the ball and through the sand.

BUNKER SHOTS

When the ball is lying on top of the sand in a bunker 10 yards or more from a green, you'd better play a pitch shot with an 8- or 9-iron instead of using your wedge and going into the sand. Play the shot off your left heel with your stance open. Your hands should be ahead of the ball at address. That will make reasonably sure that you will hit the ball correctly before taking a little divot of sand. Keep your weight accented on your left side and have the feeling that you are swinging from your left shoulder – with your left elbow straight, of course.

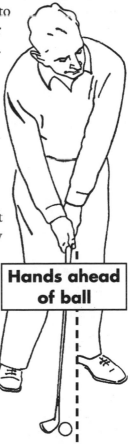

Hands ahead of ball

WEDGE SHOTS

Let the wedge do what it is designed to do: shovel into and through the sand under the ball and pitch the ball up onto the green. Why get scared stiff? All you have to do is hold your left elbow straight, swing from your left shoulder, cock your wrists early in the backswing and swing the club down into the sand an inch or so in back of the ball. That "inch or so in back of the ball gives you a big margin of error. So just stand easy and steady and swing the wedge. It will do the rest. Let the club complete its job and go through the sand and finish high.

Swing—let the wedge work

MORE WEDGE SHOTS

When you miss a wedge shot in a trap you may be sure you were scared and hurried without the slightest reason. In the sand you aim the wedge about $1^1/2$ inches in back of the ball. Keep your head steady and you've got nothing to worry about with that margin of error allowable. You've got to keep swinging so the wedge goes through the sand under the ball and comes out and up with a good follow-through. Be slow, almost lazy, in the swing. Cock your wrists as you begin your backswing and have the feeling that the butt end of the shaft is being pulled toward the ball in the down-swing before you uncock your wrists.

Don't stop!

SAND TRAP SHOTS

Play your sand trap shots in a lazy tempo. Often the average golfer gets panicky, hurries and dubs those wedge shots that really are the easiest of all shots to make well. All you have to do is: (1) Swing with your left arm straight. (2) Cock your wrists as you start your backswing. (3) Keep your head steady and keep looking at the spot in back of the ball where you want to hit the wedge into the sand. (4) Follow through so your wedge will go through the sand under the ball and bring the ball up and out as the sand is shoveled up.

Go through the sand!

SPECIAL SITUATION SHOTS

LONGER IRON CLUBS

The ordinary golfer is afraid to use the longer iron clubs. He lacks confidence in them, often because he forgets that the shaft of the long iron club is 4 or 5 inches shorter than that of woods other than the 5-wood. Hence, he's got to play the long iron with his hands closer to his body than they are when he plays the woods. It would surprise many golfers to learn that the loft of a 3-iron is approximately 23 degrees, which is about the loft of a 5-wood. Yet the average player thinks the 3-iron is so straight-faced he will have difficulty getting the ball up, though with a 5-wood the ball will come up without being scooped.

Lowest point of swing

OUT OF THE ROUGH

Take it a little easier and you'll get out of the rough better. The tendency is to grab the club tightly and try to cut the ball out, but then you stiffen completely and the rough slows down your club. Hold the club (mainly with your fingers, of course) firmly but gently so you can hit down with an 8- or 9-iron into thick rough and pop the ball up and out. If the ball is lying high on a mat of tangled rough and you want some distance, take a 4-wood. Hit with your hands and resist the inclination to throw yourself at the shot, thinking that brute force will get the ball out. Use your head in deciding whether you are one or two shots from the green when you're in the rough.

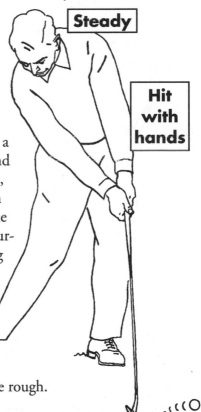

Steady

Hit with hands

TIPS FROM SENIORS

Playing winter vacation golf with senior golfers, whose smart and nimble brains offset the aging of their muscles, I get refresher lessons in chipping close enough for one easy putt. These old boys who take my money do carefully what helped me win championships but which I am inclined to do carelessly now. They always (1) have their weight very emphatically on the left foot at address and keep it there all during the stroke; (2) have an open stance, halfway facing the hole at address, with the right foot square to the direction line so they'll get an upright swing; and (3) address the ball even with the right toe, with their hands well ahead of it.

Weight accented on left foot

STRAIGHT LEFT ARM

Better keep your left hand definitely in control of the club and keep it moving through the shot or you'll be out of luck on the short chips and pitches. Keep your weight quite positively on your left foot so you will hit down and connect solidly and accurately.

The last three fingers of your left hand must be in command of the club and your straight left arm has got to swing toward the hole. Should your right hand boss the shot it probably will roll over the left hand as you are hitting and you'll make a mess of the job. The right hand supplies the "touch" that measures the power you need for these short approaches.

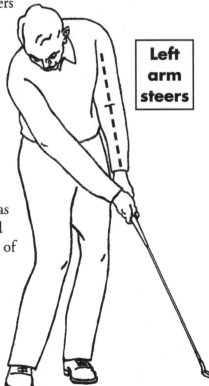

Left arm steers

OUT OF THE SAND

Golf's easiest shot is with a wedge out of the sand onto the adjacent green. You don't hit the ball at all, but swing the wedge into the sand an inch or two in back of the ball. The sand throws the ball up and out. Keep swinging so the club goes under the ball and follows through without being "braked." When the ball is lying fairly well in the sand play the shot with an open stance and the ball about in line off the left heel. Cock your wrists quickly in the backswing. Keep your left elbow straight and your right elbow down. There's very little body action in this shot so keeping your head steady is easy.

Keep swinging

VACATION LIES

The winter vacation golfer in the South, Southwest or Hawaii will get plenty of lies on thin turf or in sand just off the fairway. Those shots can improve his game greatly because to play them with any results at all he's got to hit down at the ball. That will get the ball up and on its way. If he tries to scoop it up he is completely out of luck. Shots from close lies you've got to play with the ball a little to the right of your left heel; almost to the center of your stance. Lift your left hand high in the backswing and keep your right elbow down and close to your ribs, so you will be whipping the club down almost as though you wanted to hit the ball into the ground.

Hit down

LOOSEN UP

If you have learned anything by observation you have learned that the professionals do not practice as the average player does. The pros practice something specific. Amateurs merely hit shots without concentration on one particular point. For instance: Do you concentrate when you practice chipping? You've got to put every chip within six feet of the hole (that gives you a 12-foot diameter) or you are inexcusably careless with grip, stance, aim and swing. If you have been reading my tutoring you know how to make every golf shot that is needed. If you do not make the shot you are either careless or too tense. Loosen up; golf is a pleasure, not an ordeal.

Think of precision

IRON SHOTS

The typical golfer doesn't use his 3-, 4- or 5-iron well (or often enough) because he tries to scoop those shots up. Then he tops them and loses confidence in the clubs. He should address those shots with the ball about midway between the feet and his hands slightly ahead of the ball. His knees ought to be slightly bent at address so he can turn freely and stay in balance. It's very important that his right elbow stay down and comfortably close to his ribs as he turns and that his left elbow stay straight. These things help him get a fairly upright swing so he can whip the club into the shot and get the leading edge of the club under the ball at the bottom of the arc of the swing.

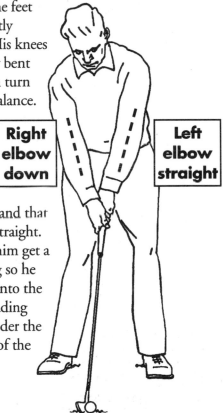

Right elbow down

Left elbow straight

HANDS AHEAD

Often the average golfer tops his pitch shots or hits them far to the left of the target. Usually these errors result from reaching for the ball. Sole the pitching club behind the ball and have your hands close to your body as you get your stance. At address your hands should be ahead of the ball so your left arm and the shaft slant back toward the ball, which should be a bit to the right of the center of your stance. Have your chin up a trifle and steady so you can swing your shoulders under it. With that address and a straight left arm you are almost certain to get the leading edge of the club going under the ball and squarely along the direction line.

Don't 'reach' for the ball

THE CHIP SHOT

The chip shot is virtually a lofted putt from off the green that runs toward the hole. Play it carefully and it will save you a stroke. Take a slightly firmer finger hold down on the grip of the club. Keep your head absolutely still. Unlock your knees. You can break your wrists a little but by all means swing your left arm with the elbow straight and with your right elbow tucked to your side. Keep your hands in close to you. This will have you controling the club with your left arm and hand. If the right hand takes command you are ruined.

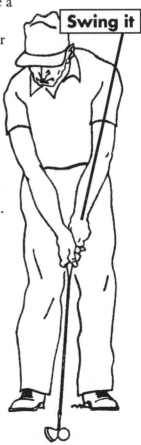

Swing it

CLUB LOFTS

It surprises many golfers to learn that the loft of a 5-wood is about 23 degrees and that the lofting angle of the face of a 3-iron also is 23 degrees. But the ordinary golfer can get the ball up in the air well with a 5-wood when he can hardly get it off the ground with a 3-iron. The reason usually is that the face of the 5-wood is just far enough ahead of the shaft to compensate for the lifting action the average golfer erroneously tries to put into a shot. He has got to hit down correctly and get the leading edge of the club under the ball when he is using the 3-iron.

Hit down

A WINTER TIP

A great thing about winter golf, whether it's indoors in the North or outside in a vacation atmosphere in the South, is that you can attend more to yourself instead of the main problem being beating somebody else. In the winter you can concentrate on your shot-making technique. In the case of the ordinary golfer that means working on his short game. From 100 yards to the hole, the average golfer wastes six or more strokes that he could have saved by getting in the habit of swinging from his left shoulder in making the easy, smooth and delicate pitch and chip shots. One essential thing about making these shots correctly is to address the ball with weight mainly on the left foot, keeping it there throughout the swing.

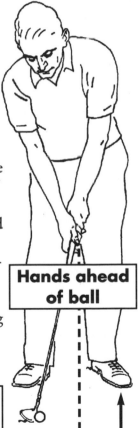

Hands ahead of ball

Weight accented on left foot

TIPS
FOR
WOMEN

STAY BEHIND THE BALL

Sometimes the woman golfer doesn't know what is meant when she is urged to "stay behind the ball." This illustration explains the advice. It means that she should start her downswing by planting her left foot solidly on the ground, then pull down her club with her straight left arm without allowing her head to change position. She ought to keep her nose pointing a bit to the right of the ball until her right shoulder gets well under her chin and her hands go out after the ball.

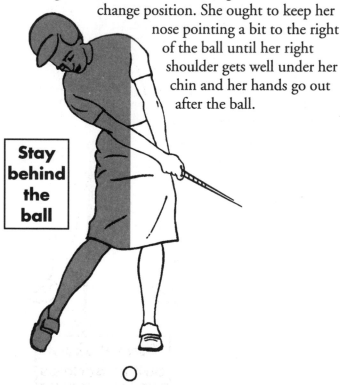

Stay behind the ball

FEMININE ERRORS

M ost women golfers would hit many good shots
and fewer bad ones if they would correct the
common bad habit of having the
ball too far to the left at address.
I see a lot of women from 16 to
60 making the error of having
the ball ahead of the line off
the left toe. Then they've got
to fall into the shot instead of
standing up with the head
steady and swinging and
whipping the clubhead into
the ball. The average woman
golfer misuses a tremendous
amount of effort on a shot.
Not enough of that effort is
with the hands at the
critical bottom part of
the swing.

**Careful about
ball at address**

HANDS SLIGHTLY AHEAD

At address the woman golfer gives herself greater assurance of hitting her shots satisfactorily if she has her hands slightly ahead of the ball. There is an exception: When the ball is teed up for a drive, then her hands can be in about the same plane as the ball. She should have her right elbow bent in a little so it is close to her body and just about in line with her right knee. It's a good idea for her to have her right knee turned a little to the left as she addresses the ball. Then her first move will start her pivoting on her right leg instead of swaying to the right. At this address position the main thing for her to think of is swinging the club around and up with a straight left arm.

Hands ahead of ball

Make Smooth Weight Shift

Women golfers often tell me they are "hopeless" in attempting to make short shots, and I don't wonder. They misplay these shots by shifting their weight and getting too much body into what should be a smooth, unhurried swing from the shoulders and, at the last instant, a crisp smack with the hands. The weight should be accented on the left foot at address and kept there all through the swing. The hands should be well ahead of the ball in addressing these short shots.

The feet ought to be fairly close together and the ball on a line to the right of the center of the stance. The left arm should be straight and the right elbow bent down, close to the ribs and approximately above the right knee.

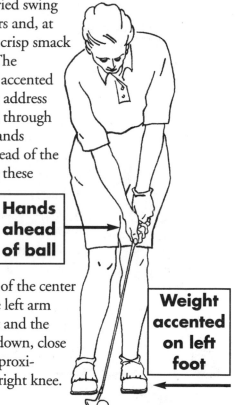

Hands ahead of ball

Weight accented on left foot

BALANCE IS KEY

One of the big "secrets" of the women who play superior golf is that they are exceptionally set in a strong, well-balanced and unlocked position at the top of the backswing. The average woman golfer is unsteady and hasn't command of the club at the top.

Note the essentials of fine style in this drawing made from a photograph of one of our greatest female players: (1) She is firm on her feet. The right foot is solidly on the ground; the inner edge of her left foot is firmly set and her left knee points to behind the ball. (2) She is braced but not rigid on her right leg. (3) Her left elbow is straight and she's looking at the ball over her left shoulder. (4) Her right elbow is down. (5) She has the last three fingers of her left hand securely in control of the club.

DON'T OVERSWING

About 9 out of 10 women golfers overswing. That might be a good thing instead of a fault if (1) they had a firm and flexible finger grip so they'd keep the club controlled and if (2) they stayed in balance so they could swing their arms and hands with correct leverage instead of swaying and falling and never getting set to hit with authority. When the woman golfer learns that she can hold the club with her fingers exactly as it should be held and doesn't have to have brute power to hit a satisfactory long shot, she enters a wonderfully pleasant stage of improvement.

Hold firm with fingers

WOMEN'S INSTINCT

Most of today's American women who play golf are instinctively qualified to score better than they do. They get too tense with technicalities, the majority of which are complications needlessly introduced by loving and bossy husbands and sweethearts. There are only a few simple essentials for the woman golfer: (1) Hold the club wrapped chiefly in the last three fingers of the left hand. (2) Stand unlocked and stably balanced. (3) Swing with 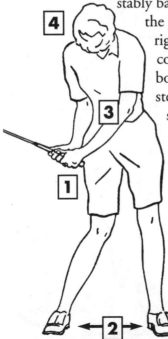 the left arm straight and the right elbow down and comfortably close to the body. (4) Keep the head steady so the shoulders swing beneath the chin and at the latest possible moment whip the club into the ball with your hands. Leave all you possibly can to women's instinctively good sense of rhythm and hand action.

PROPER TENSION

Somewhere between relaxation and tightness lies the proper degree of tension for fine golf. The typical woman golfer is too relaxed. She swings freely but weakly. Her husband is too tense. At address he holds the club almost hard enough to flatten the shaft. That stiffens his forearms, his shoulders, his hips and legs – and worst of all his brain, so he is scared stiff and forgets to hit the ball. There are three places to extablish the correct degree of tension at address: (1) in the legs by unlocking the knees; (2) in the shoulders by "unfreezing" them to swing the arms freely; and (3) in the forearms by holding the club mainly with the fingers.

GENTLE GRIP

The majority of women golfers hold the club so deadly tight they stiffen their forearms and shoulders and every other part of the body. Then they can't do anything else but heave themselves at the ball instead of hitting it with their hands. Press the club grip against the heel of the left hand with the tips of the last three fingers of that hand and the club will be held so securely it needn't be clutched in a frozen, inflexible connection. A gentle hold with the fingers of the right hand, with the hands placed closely together, **Firm** completes the coupling that allows the woman golfer to whip life into the shot.

Gentle

HITTING HARD

The typical woman golfer seldom hits the ball as hard as she can and should. Usually she hammers at the ball. Her weakness is in her method. She needs to hold her club mainly with the last three fingers of her left hand and the middle two of her right so she can whip the club into the shot. She also should hold her left elbow straight so her extended left arm swings the club accurately to where she can confidently hit with her hands. She should unlock her knees and sit down a bit to the shot so she can turn her body while keeping her head steady.

Straight left arm

Fingers hold club

Knees unlocked

SHOULDER ERRORS

When I see a woman golfer with a smear of lipstick on the shoulder of her blouse I can tell her the answer to her trouble the instant she asks me. She is turning her shoulders too much in a horizontal plane instead of having them swing under and around her chin. She's probably standing too erect instead of bending at the knees, "sitting down" slightly and bending from the shoulders as she addresses the ball. The error of that flat turn of the shoulders is very common with men golfers as well as with women.

Shoulder swings under chin

STRAIGHT APPROACH SHOTS

Often men and women will complain to me about their approach shots going to the left of the target. I can cure that trouble without leaving the clubhouse. What they are doing is moving the right shoulder in a nearly horizontal plane – "over the ball" is the pro's term for the error. They should adjust the swing so it is more upright than flat, so the right elbow stays close to the ribs and the right shoulder comes under the chin. Then they'll hit those shots straight instead of steering them to the left.

Shoulder under chin

Swing more upright